About the Authors

ROBERTA MARTIN STARRY has explored, painted, photographed, and written about the California, Arizona, Nevada and Oregon backcountry for the past 50 years. She also gave lectures and tours for students, youth groups, and museum members on the history, geology and flora of the eastern Kern County. Now retired, Roberta Martin Starry had for many years been the Rand area correspondent for *The Bakersfield Californian*. A member of Western Writers of America, she was also a free-lance writer with articles and photos appearing in many national publications including: *The West, Collector's World, National Park Magazine, Mother Earth News* and *American Gold News*. Articles and photos were used by regional publications including: *Desert Magazine, Nevada and California Supplements*. Through the years, her photographs of desert subjects, paintings and historical articles have won numerous awards.

SUZANNE KNUDSON is by training an anthropologist, with a specialization in historical archaeology. Currently a community college professor, she has also traveled extensively throughout the United States, and has visited historic sites around the world. She has done field work in the Middle East, Utah, Virginia and California, and has conducted summer educational programs for secondary education students at historic sites in Virginia. She is presently involved in an historical survey of the Carson and Colorado railroad right of way, and in an historic restoration project in the ghost town of Garlock, California.

Front Cover: Picture of Randsburg today.

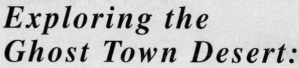

Exploring the Ghost Town Desert:
A Guide to the Rand Mining Area, its Natural and Historic Points of Interest

by Roberta Martin Starry
with
Suzanne Knudson

Dedicated to Edwin S. Martin,
the desert explorer *par excellence*

Editor: Tom Woods

Book and cover design by Casa Graphics, Inc.

Photographs: Authors' collection, except where noted

Copyright © 2000 by Engler Publishing
    Engler Publishing is an imprint of
    George N. Engler & Associates

Portions of this edition previously copyrighted in 1973 by
    Roberta Martin Starry and Published by Ward Ritchie Press

Printed in the United States of America

Gem Guides Book Co.
315 Cloverleaf Drive, Suite F
Baldwin Park, CA 91706

Library of Congress Catalog Card Number: 99-75639
International Standard Book Number: 0-9674637-0-X

~ CONTENTS ~

ENJOY YOURSELF — DISCLAIMER

We hope this book provides you and your family with some interesting hours of desert exploring. Please remember that neither this book nor any other can really prepare you totally for the wonders or possible dangers of desert travel. As we have tried to point out in various parts of the text, there are always potential problems one may encounter on the backroads. Flash floods, washed-out roads, flat tires, overheated radiators, and unanticipated problems of other sorts are things only your own good common sense and caution can prepare you for in your explorations, for help may be a long way off. The authors and the publisher of this book disclaim any and all liability for any damage to the cars or injury to the people who attempt these trips.

Introduction

The 1848 discovery of gold at John Sutter's mill in Coloma, California heralded the California gold rush. It also spawned other searches for gold in California and created a frenzy of mining in California's high Mojave Desert region north of the San Gabriel mountain range in Southern California. In reality, miners trudged their way through this region since the early 1800s and there's much to show for it. This vast, picturesque, yet desolate region not only produced its share of mining history, but it has left fascinating stories of booms and busts, and given today's vacationer and explorer rich legends and territories to explore.

isecting the historic Rand Mining area is U.S. Highway 395, approximately 150 miles north of Los Angeles, and serves as the main street of the diminutive communities of Atolia, Red Mountain and Johannesburg. Randsburg, where the big mining boom originated, is but a short distance off the highway seen clinging to the mountainside below the one time great gold producing Yellow Aster Mine.

The Rand area in the Mojave Desert has an exciting yet well-balanced mixture of sand, rock, rugged mountain ranges and colorful canyons interlaced with old trails, abandoned prospects and crumbling buildings. Through each mile runs an invisible tread that ties the present to a romantic past of freighters, prospectors, investors, gamblers and pretty dance hall girls.

Adventure Ahead

The flavor of those old days is still around, in a lesser degree as the years pass, but for those who pause to look, listen and feel, there is an illusive something from back in time. Adventure waits just around the curve of a dusty trail and challenging mountains hold wealth yet to be discovered.

Over 100 years ago prospectors hiked and rock sampled their way along the foothills and canyons of the mineralized El Paso Mountains. Their search did not always produce gold but it did compensate with ability to survive in an arid land, outwit the lawless and add to the understanding of geology. It was a lonely life measured against today's standards.

The first exciting gold discovery to draw public attention to this area was made in a gulch opening into Fremont Valley, on the eastern side of the El Paso Range. Forty-four years earlier, an emigrant named Goler had seen nuggets somewhere in this locality while making his way from Death Valley to the Los Angeles area. Starved, weak, and frightened of Indians, Goler hurried south, with plans of someday returning to claim the gold. Investors believed the story and financed several searches, none with any degree of success.

The narrow canyon of the 1893 strike became known as Goler. There were those that believed it was the lost gold site. Others passed the idea off as miner's talk and went on searching for a bigger strike. Whether Goler saw this place or not was of little concern as excitement over the find mounted. Glamour of the Mother Lode in northern California was about gone and prospectors were frantically searching for a rich new field.

News of Gold

Word of the strike spread fast, men arrived in droves and grabbed any claim they could get. Considering the slow transportation of that time, plus the total lack of phones or other means of communication, the speed with which news of gold traveled is still one of the unexplained wonders of the desert. Miners of the early Rand years credit the sage brush telegraph and jack rabbit gossip for the fast news coverage.

Restlessness, a characteristic of prospectors, was probably the greatest factor in new discoveries. Summit Diggings a few miles to the east of Goler was producing well but prospectors moved back and forth between the two camps always searching for that big bonanza.

In 1895 three men who had periodically moved between the Goler and Summit operations decided to make one last search for gold before quitting their profitless mining venture. They left the Summit Diggings after telling friends that they were going to make one more try on their Goler claims but actually turned west toward a mountain that had been bypassed by prospectors as showing no sign of mineralization.

Randsburg around 1902.

Mountain Millionaires

For F.M. Mooers, John Singleton and Charles Burcham, their last prospecting effort was their best. The colorless, uninteresting mountain made them millionaires.

At the first sign of gold the three prospectors had fanatically set about staking as many claims as possible before anyone learned of the discovery. Like Goler it was only a matter of a few hours before men began arriving, marking off claims and setting up their camps.

Rand Camp started as one tent, but quickly progressed to a tent, wagon-box and board city that burned to the ground twice within a few weeks. Undaunted by lack of water, primitive living conditions, and baffling desert weather, men poured in and a boom was on. High pitched laughter and piano music echoed in the saloon-lined streets, competing with lodge meetings and opera-house entertainment.

Down in Fremont Valley a small settlement known as Cow Wells had been little more than a cow watering place and a way station for freighters on the long haul to and from the Panamint mines west of Death Valley. Goler and Rand Camp's Yellow Aster gold, hauled to Eugene Garlock's mill at Cow Wells, created a boom in the settlement that was eventually renamed Garlock. It became a favored rest stop for miner, businessman, greenhorn, gambler or family enroute to the gold fields. Hotels offered good beds, home cooked food, and the latest gold news. Saloons washed away the dust of stage coach miles, a rough freight wagon trip or a long hike in from the mountains with a poke of gold. Corrals and stables housed weary teams while drivers relaxed. A one man laundry kept the miners clean and a slaughter house provided the whole area with fresh meat, as fresh as a team and wagon could manage to deliver.

Here Today . . . Then Gone!

Prosperity had arrived only to be snatched away when the Yellow Aster mine built its own mill. The big ore wagons no longer skidded down the steep Rand grade and lugged across the sandy valley to the Garlock mills. Everything moved toward Rand Mountain where a rail line was coming in from San Bernardino, water was being piped from a spring to the east, and there were mine jobs for those who did not work their own claim. Men, business and buildings moved to Randsburg.

Johannesburg, a planned town just around the mountain from Randsburg, had its mills, stores, and saloons and boasted about its orderly growth compared to the haphazard Rand Camp. Its golf course, 9 holes played around the boundary of the town, was a rare desert refinement that lent prestige to the community. Lively rivalry between Johannesburg and Randsburg existed for years and was probably sparked by the fact that the Randsburg Railroad stopped at Johannesburg and never did get around the mountain to the larger town.

Long before gold was discovered in the Rand Mountains, Red Rock Canyon to the west had become a route south for explorers and the remnant of '49ers that had survived Death Valley. By the late 1860s, deep, worn ruts had developed. Wagons, heavy with bullion from the Cerro Gordo silver mine, were churning the deep sand and leaving dust trails between the wind-and-water-sculptured walls of the canyon. Lone miners working the side washes waved at the passing drivers or came out to hear the latest news. An occasional big nugget teased the miners into staying and had the outside world watching for a new bonanza to develop.

Colorful as the canyon was, an emigrant named Koehn, who pedaled his bicycle through the valley enroute to the Panamint mines saw the need for a rest stop for travelers. He gave up his plans to reach the mines and built a way-station near a spring in view of Red Rock's red-and-pink-topped cliffs. When gold was discovered in Goler, Koehn was one of the first to arrive and brought a wagon load of supplies including supplies for the first bar.

The Welcome Wagon

Koehn started a delivery route as mining increased and his wagon with food, dynamite, picks, shovels and mail was a welcome sight around Goler, Summit and the diggings all over Rand Mountain. His way-station became a favored stage stop where news of the mines was as recent as the delivery wagon's last trip.

When a big mining boom is over most associated communities fade away. Randsburg and Johannesburg were no exceptions. Men left for better pay, families moved away, and buildings became empty. Signs of the end chilled the mountain communities. Then a new lease on life came in the form of a tungsten discovery in 1905. At first there was only rumor, then came a railroad siding, and finally men were being hired. The Rand area was off on another bonanza that lasted until the demands of World War I were met. The price of tungsten dropped and the mines closed.

The outlook was bleak. Very little gold was being processed and tungsten was finished. That hundreds of miners had been walking over high grade silver for years, came as a surprise in 1919 when two prospectors recognized the metal. A whole new show went into production about halfway between the Randsburg-Johannesburg gold fields and Atolia's tungsten.

Empty buildings became desirable property and movers went to work. Every usable structure was transported to a site near the new find and still the surge of miners outstripped the available housing. Miners and their families made do with tents, houses still on moving blocks, and shacks thrown together out of junk materials.

Twin Towns

Two communities developed within a few yards of each other. One was Osdick named for a miner who held claims at the site and the other was known by a number of names including Inn City and Sin City. Postal department problems ended only after they disregarded the names heaped upon the two feuding communities and they designated the post office as Red Mountain. There was local resentment over the postal department's decision, but by any name it was a wild place.

Early buildings of the Yellow Aster Mine, 1899 - 1902.

Red Mountain became well known as a wide open town where one could get a drink in any place of business except the post office. The madams were proud of their high-class houses, and the girls were most attractive. Prohibition had little effect as warnings came ahead of the raids, and the town turned temporarily dry. Shootings were hushed up and soon forgotten. The town was lively on week nights, but on Saturday night the place roared. Bands came from Los Angeles to play through the night and out of town crowds arrived to join in the fun or watch the show. Long after the silver boom was over, Red Mountain lived on as an old-west type night spot.

Until recently, there was only limited mining activity, but old timers continued to look for the new boom and at times their hopes were fanned by rumors. There was the year government men combed the old tunnels of the Yellow Aster to see if it would be suitable for storing valuable documents. It would have been a multi-million dollar deal, a boost to the community, and jobs for men. But the tunnels were too deteriorated to reclaim. There was a later rumor that revolved around Randsburg becoming a tourist attraction with luxury swimming pools, motels, ore train trips and "packaged recreation" in an old mining town atmosphere. Then, in 1984, rumor became reality when The Rand Mining Company, a subsidiary of Glamis Gold, Inc. of Canada acquired the old Yellow Aster Mine and turned it into a large open pit mining operation. Randsburg is once again an active mining town, at least until the next "bust."

From Rumor to Reality

This is the way of things in the ghost town desert of the Rand Mining District. One never knows when the next rumor may turn into the real thing and a slumbering camp will spring to life once more. So, before the next boom changes the face of things yet again, the ghost town explorer should become acquainted with the Rand. It is easy to reach from either Highway 395 or 14. Visitors will need to have their own sleeping accommodations or plan to stay overnight in one of the two (at present) bed and breakfast inns in the area or at motels in Four-Corners, Ridgecrest, Trona or Mojave, an approximately thirty mile drive to any one of them.

Randsburg has a general store, three facilities serving food, two bars, several antique stores, bottle shops, and a museum. Johannesburg has a couple of curio shops. Red Mountain has two antique shops. There are no businesses in Atolia, Garlock, Goler or Cantil. There are no gas stations in any of these communities. The closest stations are in California City, Four-Corners, Mojave, Ridgecrest or Trona.

Comfortable exploration of the desert, back roads and mining communities is best confined to three seasons. Spring is beautiful with multi-color flowers and the air carries their light perfume of subtle mixtures. Fall is gold, tan and mauve against moving clouds. Winter, a time of varied moods, can quickly change from warm to cold, sunny to cloudy, and darkness comes early in the canyons. Summers are hot, and not the best time to explore the back country or climb mountains.

There is something to enjoy for almost everyone in the Rand area. Without leaving hard surfaced roads there are ghost towns, abandoned mine camps, former ranch country and two museums that tell the mining story. Dirt roads, passable for SUVs and passenger cars, offer old landmarks that were the road signs for pioneers, gold diggings where one can pan out some "colors" the early miners passed up in their rush to greater riches, and scattered small camps where relics and bottles may be found. There is a safe tunnel that goes through a mountain, scenic canyons, Indian camp sites and former ranching projects to visit. Beyond passenger car limits are freighter trails, mines, remains of Chinese camps and diggings, plus rock, bottle and relic collecting.

Color, Color Everywhere

Line, color and form challenge the artist and photographer everywhere. History devotees have freight and borax routes to map, long forgotten way stations to locate, and ruins to identify. Railroad buffs can hike the old shoo-fly used when Southern Pacific built north to meet the Carson and Colorado's narrow gage. Only the roadbed of the Randsburg Railroad is left and one water tank still stands at the ruins of Searles Station.

Plant and wild life is abundant in spite of the popular belief that the desert is without life. Rare plants exist in this region where an arid Death Valley band blends into an increasingly moist belt to the west. Animals, birds, reptiles and rodents make their year round home here, but seldom appear for public viewing; therein lies their survival.

Take a day, a week, a lifetime, and poke around the old diggings. Pan some gold, collect the beauty in rock or on film, discover the flowers that grow close to the ground with blooms no larger than a pin head, inhale the aroma of sage and greasewood after a desert shower. With eyes and mind join the raven as it glides on the air waves—free, relaxed and in tune with the desert world.

The Preacher and the Prospector

There is so much to experience in the Rand area that it reminds one of an old miner's story about a traveling preacher. Word was sent ahead to announce a preaching date at a point half way between Summit and Goler diggings. Either the word didn't get around or the miners were too busy because no one showed up.

The preacher was about to give up waiting when he was delighted to see a lone prospector and burro coming along the narrow trail. After welcoming the ragged, bearded man the preacher went right into his sermon, which went on and on. The burro's ears drooped and the prospector sagged in his tracks. Finally the preacher paused and asked, "Now, how was that for a sermon?"

The old prospector slowly adjusted the burro's pack, then turned to the preacher and said, "If I had a whole load of hay, I'd feed my burro a little. I wouldn't give him the whole load at one time!"

This guide book is just a taste of what the Rand area has to offer. If you want the whole load there are volumes to read, old records to search and miles to explore after you have made an acquaintance with this historic and fascinating area of California.

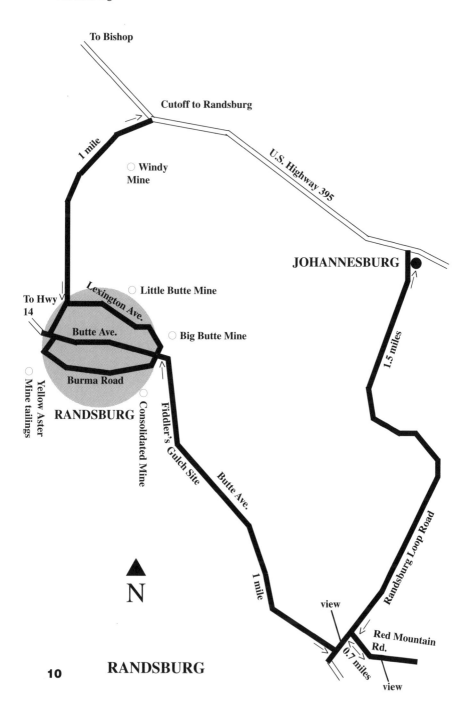

To Bishop

Cutoff to Randsburg

1 mile

○ Windy Mine

U.S. Highway 395

JOHANNESBURG

To Hwy 14

Lexington Ave.

○ Little Butte Mine

Butte Ave.

○ Big Butte Mine

Burma Road

○ Yellow Aster Mine tailings

RANDSBURG

○ Consolidated Mine

Fiddler's Gulch Site

Butte Ave.

1 mile

1.5 miles

Randsburg Loop Road

view

Red Mountain Rd.

0.7 miles

view

▲
N

RANDSBURG

Randsburg

A visit to this old gold camp that produced millionaires can be made year 'round by any type of vehicle. Summer heat is not prohibitive at the altitude of 3500 feet.

Want to stroll across a secret tunnel, examine the bullet holes left from a saloon brawl, stand at a bank window where gold headed the deposit slip, have an old-fashioned soda at an authentic vintage fountain or view the picturesque eroded tailings of one of Southern California's richest mines? Get in the mood by mentally stepping back to the time when three men discovered gold on the side of an unnamed mountain in the Mojave Desert.

It was the spring of 1895 and they let no one know of their discovery as they hurried to lay out claims, but by the time the first corners of their claim were marked, prospectors started pouring in from every direction to stake claims for themselves. The nearest gold diggings were about ten miles away, yet the feel or knowledge of a new strike spread to even more distant camps. Old timers credited this communication phenomenon to the "sagebrush telegraph." Just how the news spread through the sparsely settled miles remains one of the desert's closely-guarded secrets.

Rand Camp, like most early day mining camps of the west, started as a sprawling tent community. Living conditions were rough and a miner was considered fortunate to have a tent, a wagon box or even a tarp to drape over bushes for a shelter. Wind vigorously worked at adding to man's discomfort. Summer heat had a way of bearing down and sapping moisture while freezing temperatures reinforced with an occasional snow was often winter fare. It was no place for the timid or weak.

Similar to other thriving mining camps, one of the first business places was a tent saloon furnished with a plank bar and a few makeshift card tables on the side. The tables relieved the miner from the burden of carrying his heavy gold around with him and the bar provided fuel to fire him up for another go at the hard work of mining.

As Rand gold lived up to and exceeded the rumors, the camp boomed into a town of many businesses including hotels, saloons, stores and a theater. There was an atmosphere, a community personality unique to Randsburg, some of which is still there for the discerning visitor to experience.

The remains of the fascinating old camp can be reached from either Highway 395 or 14 via hard-surfaced roads that converge at the edge of town and swing into Butte Avenue. Your first impression of Randsburg is that it is a movie or television set using false-front buildings. However, the buildings are not make believe. They are real and their life story reaches far back before the flicks or the tube.

Where to Start

The general store, easily identifiable on the right side of the street is an ideal point from which to start exploring. Before going in, take a look at the former post office which is the adjacent building to the right. The thick adobe walls were built as protection against the many disastrous fires that hit the dry camp before the turn of the century. The walls stood through the holocausts but the roof was replaced a number of times. The building had many lives, both good and not so good, before gaining respectability in its recent service to the community. In spite of its small size the building served for a number of years as a rooming house where the beds never got cold. When one miner went to work another came in to sleep. There were three shifts at the mine and three shifts to each bed.

On the right side of the old post office is a building that served as union headquarters for the battle waged by the miner's union in its effort to organize the Yellow Aster Mine on the hill above town. That was a period of near disaster for the mine. Fires were set in the tunnels, fights erupted and men were out of work. It was a time when there were two Saturday night dances, one union, one non-union. Union men were not allowed to dance with a girl that had been at the nonunion dance, but women were in short supply and there was active stealing of girls from one dance to the other.

On the left side of the one-time post office is the general store which stocks everything from patent medicines to miner's lights and gold pans just as it did back in boom times. Toward the back of the store is a soda fountain where years ago the famous ice cream creation "The Gondola" and the miner's after-work drink, "Salty Joe" were born. Visitors today, served at the same fountain, can enjoy old-fashioned cold drinks and thick sodas while studying the true-to-life action in an oil painting hanging over the mirrored back bar. The general store serves breakfast and lunch daily.

Though the once rowdy White House Saloon across the street no longer serves Flusseys (three shots of whiskey) for 25 cents, it is a most interesting place to visit. Today's White House Saloon has a full service bar and serves lunches and drinks to visitors on the weekends. While you relax in the old White House Saloon, perhaps you will hear an echo or two from the past, the faint tinkle of glasses, the soft laughter of the girls, the muffled slap of cards, and the stomp of miners' heavy boots silenced by the whine of bullets.

Evidence of Disagreement

The massive bar was built by Yellow Aster carpenters. Bullet holes in the walls attest to disagreements among the customers and the old cash register knew well the story of miners separated from their hard-earned gold. There was a huge dumb-waiter that carried food orders from the restaurant in the basement to the bar patrons. Below street level was not only a busy restaurant, but an ice house and a wine cellar that supplied the other businesses in town. Along the stairway from the street to the restaurant was a door that has long been boarded up. Beyond the door was a tunnel heading up the hill toward the Yellow Aster Mine and its gold. It is believed some highgrading went on through this tunnel, but it was known best as a sanctuary for individuals hiding from the law.

The roof above the bar was recessed and served as a place for the girls to entertain gentlemen on nights when high temperatures made it too uncomfortable inside the buildings. Back of the old White House, on the next street level down, are a few shacks left over from the extensive red light district that was a part of the struggling young mining camp. The girls added a touch of refinement to an almost totally male population. Laughter, love, discouragement and death, like the old tunes played on the piano in the corner, were real-life episodes played within the walls of the 30 saloons up and down the long street. Randsburg wasn't as rowdy as some mining camps are reported to have been, but it was far from a dull place. The metal shutters, still in place on the front and sides of the White House were not for looks. They were installed as insurance against stray bullets hitting a patron when street fights were common.

Though the fancy-dressed girls and the four-a-day stage coaches arriving in a cloud of dust are gone, there is still a lot of gold mining going on in another bar called "The Joint." Old timers used to say that more and bigger gold was dug along the bar of a saloon than ever saw the light of day at the end of a pick and shovel.

On up Butte Avenue are bottle and relic shops where the discards of yesterday become the treasures of today. Variety is in evidence on every shelf and information on age or former contents are free for the asking.

That's Inedible!

A picnic-rest area next to the museum is a pleasant spot to pause, relax and view the buildings lining the long street. Study the equipment, mine locomotive, working parts of a stamp mill and other artifacts rescued from abandoned mines. The first thing that the visitor sees upon entering the museum, which is open weekends, is a unique dinner of rocks that are so realistic in shape and color that they appear edible.

There is an old barber shop and gas station next door to the museum. Farther up the street, on the opposite side is an imposing building that housed the Randsburg Bank, a general store and a furniture store. A little further up the street on the left-hand side opposite the new fire station is the old Opera House. The building today houses the Randsburg Post Office and the Opera House Cafe. The cafe is open Fridays through Sundays from 8 am to 2 pm and offers breakfast and lunch. However, dinner is served on the first Saturday of each month, September through June, from 5 pm to 8 pm. Periodically, special dinner events are held on Saturday nights.

Still further up the street on the left is the Cottage Hotel Bed and Breakfast. The hotel's rooms have been restored to reflect that "By Gone Era." For reservations and information call (760) 374-2285.

Follow Butte Avenue to Burma Road where you will see the Catholic Church on the left. The other old building cornering on Butte and Burma Roads was Randsburg's first printing office. At this point turn right up Burma Road. On the left of the first curve is a small house with gingerbread trim. It was the camp's first school building. Burma Road climbs to an area that has only a few dwellings compared to the old days, but gives a good view of the present community, which is only a ghost of the original robust mining camp.

A dirt road cuts off to the left as Burma Road starts back down to Butte Avenue. This was the entrance route to the Yellow Aster Mine and along it were the homes of the mine owners and the company office. Fire, wind and the years have taken a toll. The office building is collapsing and only one home remains intact. The road is rough, there is no turning around point and the gate to the mining property is locked. This is a good vantage point to view the small remnant of tailings from the old Yellow Aster Mine, mounds and slopes of yellow sand slowly being engulfed by the ever growing new mountain of tailings produced by current Rand Mining Company activities.

Upon returning to Butte Avenue go left a few feet and then right, down a hill past the recently restored jail and turn right onto Lexington. This street is lined with homes that housed the early mining families. Exteriors have changed little but a majority have modern, comfortable interiors with interesting room combinations and split levels where cabins were moved together to form a house.

Skeletons from the Past

Across the wash from this residential area can be seen the weathered, picturesque skeleton of the Little Butte Mine buildings. As you proceed up the street you will pass on the right the Lexington street entrance to the Cottage Hotel Bed and Breakfast. When Lexington enters Butte Avenue, turn left. The big mine operation on the hill straight ahead is the Big Butte Mine and Mill. This mill continued in operation until the late 1960s, one of the last, if not the last, gold mill in California. Before it shut down it was processing ore from California's southernmost border to its north, also from Nevada and Arizona to the east. For years the price of gold remained the same but the operating costs rose for both the mill and the miners until the closure was inevitable.

View the Big Butte from the road. The mine is on private property and it is not a place to explore without a guide. Like most old mines, the shaft is deep and dangerous, shoring and ladders are no longer safe, and cyanide, a poison to be avoided that was used in the milling process, is everywhere.

Music and Mayhem

Follow Butte Avenue around the bend on the way out of town and you are in Fiddler's Gulch. In 1896 this narrow wash was a lively place populated by men living in tents and dugouts. What went on here was strictly their business, and the elite of Rand Camp followed a hands-off policy. By day the men worked at the Yellow Aster or right in the gulch. The Big Dyke, California Mine, Maria, Dos Picannini, Hard Cash and the Miner's Dream kept a good many of the men working where they lived. At night the gulch hummed with another kind of activity. The sounds of merry-making mixed with homespun music bounced from mountainside to mountainside with now and then a pistol shot to liven things up.

A few wind-scarred, sun-baked old head frames still stand over shafts that for years have had no sounds of men at work, underground blasts, or loaded ore buckets being brought to the surface. The dugouts have slowly disappeared leaving only one here and there to testify to the occupancy of Fiddler's Gulch. Even the wind singing through the old timbers and swaying the lacy limbs of greasewood does little now to stir up a vision of what the gulch was like some 90 years ago.

A mile out of Randsburg the road makes a sharp left. To the right is a dirt road leading to the main entrance of the Rand Mining

Company, a subsidiary of Glamis Gold, Inc. Within a few feet, a dirt trail takes off to the left and makes a steep climb a half mile to the mountain top. This side road is not for passenger cars but the hike to the crest is worth the exercise. The bird's eye view takes in Randsburg on one side and Johannesburg on the other; distant mountains seem so close and Telescope Peak, in Death Valley, stands out sharp and beautiful. Whether you take the dirt trail to the top of the mountain or stay on the road, this is a good place to view part of the Rand Mining Company operation. In 1984 the Rand Mining Company acquired the rights to mine the surrounding area. Tunneling is no longer used in this area in favor of open pit mining. Entire mountains are being moved from one location to another. On average, 68,000 tons of earth are moved each day.

Another view of the mining operation is just around the corner. Continue a little further on Butte to an intersection where the Randsburg Loop turns to the left and Red Mountain Road to the right. Take the Red Mountain Road 0.7 miles to a dirt road on the right that has a sign saying "Point of Interest." The dirt road climbs a hill to a lookout point where you can look back on the massive Baltic Mine Project. The entire set of mountains in front of you are part of this project. Three large plaques describe the Randsburg area, the Baltic Mine Project and the Carbon Absorption Process that is used here in processing the gold. The hill to the right is a large leach field. Periodically, the Rand Mining Company gives tours of this massive mining operation. This is done in conjunction with major events that occur in town such as Randsburg's centennial celebration.

Return to the road, going back to the intersection with the Randsburg Loop Road. Continue on the Randsburg Loop Road, dropping down into the town of Johannesburg. Turn right on The Rand Street and go down the hill to Highway 395. Turn left at the highway and within a mile the cutoff to Randsburg means another left branch. Up on the mountain, silhouetted against the sky, is the Windy Mine. The name is appropriate for there is plenty of wind day after day, except down in the mine.

Like the secret tunnel crossing the main street and the tin strewn mountain side, other remnants of the gold boom days wait to be discovered by those who have the time to explore.

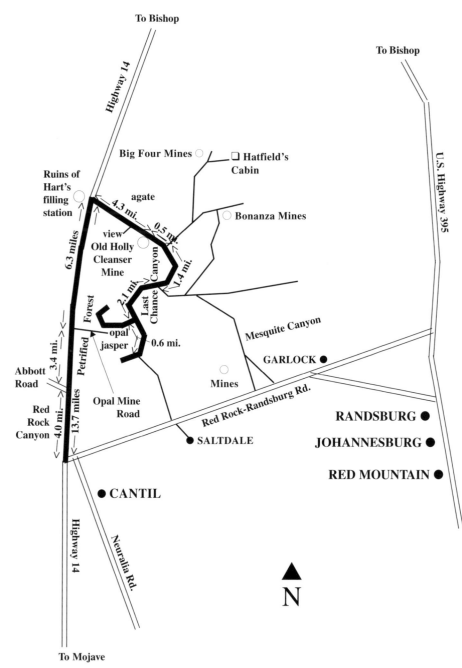

LAST CHANCE CANYON

Last Chance Canyon

Mid-October to June is the time of year to experience this canyon of scenic beauty, geological caprice and human escapades. The roads are accessible to high clearance two-wheel as well as four-wheel drive vehicles.

The route into Last Chance Canyon that most frequently appears on maps and rockhound guides shows the road branching off Red Rock-Randsburg Road. Avoid it! Never an easy trail to travel, it now has deep washes to cross; parts of the road bed are gone and the narrow, blind curves are not improving.

Instead of turning east at the junction of Highway 14 and Red Rock-Randsburg Road (if driving from Mojave), continue on Highway 14 heading north through Red Rock Canyon. Four miles north of the junction is Abbott Road which is the turnoff to the Red Rock Canyon State Park Ranger Station, visitor center and campground. Turning left on Abbott Road and crossing the south bound lanes of Highway 14, the Ranger Station is 0.7 miles ahead on a paved road. If you plan to camp in Last Chance Canyon, you need to stop at the Ranger Station to get information about the designated camp areas within the canyon. All of Last Chance Canyon is within the boundaries of Red Rock Canyon State Park. The visitor's center has interesting displays of the area and the rangers are happy to answer any questions you may have.

Going back to the highway and continuing north another 3.4 miles or 7.4 miles from the junction of Highway 14 and Red Rock-Randsburg road a sign on the right reads, "Opal Mine" a privately-owned development. For a nominal charge and only on weekends (currently $2.00 per person for ages 15 years and over) visitors can hunt for fire opal on the lower claim operated by Dick and Shirley Barnett. Road conditions vary so it is advisable to inquire at the State Park Ranger Station before attempting entrance with a passenger car. If you take this side trip, within 0.5 miles there is a road that branches off to the left. Stay on the road that angles to the right. Within another 0.2 miles another road branches off to the left. Stay on the road that angles to the right. You will go up and down hills for 2.2 miles at which point you are in a wash with a Salt Cedar tree to your right and a sign to your left directing you to turn left to the opal mine. When you turn left you will go up and down more hills for another 2.1 miles to the mine. There are signs along the way from Highway 14 leading you to the mine. For some of the signs you need to look closely for the directional arrow. For further information, you can call the Barnetts at (805) 399-7013 or write them at 1315 Castaic Ave., Bakersfield, CA 93308. Their fliers are available at the ranger station.

A Field of Agates

Thirteen and seven-tenths miles from the intersection of Highway 14 and Red Rock-Randsburg Road (33.9 miles north of Mojave), a good dirt road to the right leaves Highway 14 directly opposite the remains of Hart's filling station. The ruins of the filling station are fenced in chain link and are between the large billboard signs. When you turn right you will see a small sign saying "Schmidt Tunnel" 9 miles, a BLM road sign saying EP 15, and you will cross a cattle guard. This entrance to the canyon is well traveled and presents no problems for high clearance vehicles as long as visitors stay on the road. Avoid the soft, sandy shoulders because they are not for driving or turning around. Fawn colored landscape stretches out for three miles interrupted only by an occasional dark green Joshua. A gem-quality agate field is marked by the appearance of gray-white hills to the left. Some chunks of the material can be found by walking a short distance on either side of the road, but for good collecting continue on for a mile until nearly opposite the hills. A fair road (which is closed to vehicles) takes off to the agate field but a better one is a little further (4.3 miles from Highway 14) where an excellent dirt road crosses the main route. The left branch (which is closed to vehicles) leads a short distance to an old camping area within easy reach of the agate that appears in layers of mottled blue, pink, tan to deep caramel.

Ice Cream Sundae Country

The road to the right, opposite the one going to the agate field, as well as the one 0.1 miles back on the right stops at the rim of the canyon (0.4 miles) where there is a splendid view of pumice mining and Last Chance Canyon's strawberry, chocolate, vanilla, ice cream sundae country.

Continuing on the main road another 0.3 miles or 4.6 miles from Highway 14, the ruins of an extensive mining-milling operation comes into view on your right. It was here in the early 1930s that a prospector, who managed to divert his eyes and thoughts from gold, found a sizeable ledge of pure white pumice or volcanic ash. The discovery developed into the home of the Holly Cleanser that became a competitor of the widely advertised Dutch Cleanser which was mining similar material a few miles to the south.

The ruins are within the boundary of Red Rock Canyon State Park. When the mill was operating it produced material used in products that varied from insulation and acoustical plaster of the building trade, to oil absorbing filters, cleaning compounds and soil conditioner for golf courses. The very finest grade, that feels like silk, was used in tooth powder and polish for gold, silver, copper and chrome objects.

The road skirts left of the mill and tops a hill 0.2 miles from the ruins and 4.8 miles from Highway 14. An interesting side trip can be made by taking a sharp turn to the left following the BLM road EP 15 that runs along the ridge of the hill for 0.8 miles. Stop as the road dips toward another valley opposite a little gray cabin off on another ridge to the right.

The route ahead leads into interesting country, but the road frequently changes. One day it is excellent, and the next day after a rain, it will be a jumble of boulders. Do not attempt to travel down this grade unless you have a four-wheel drive vehicle, an ATV, a dirt bike or a high-clearance truck.

The explorer who has to turn around at this point need not go away disappointed. Scoop up a handful of the black sand at the bottom of the two tracks cut by years of travel, or get down on your knees. In either case blow gently to separate and move the black sand. Chances are there will be flakes of gold showing where the sand has been. Known as flour gold, it is so fine that a slight breeze will carry it away.

Mile-Long Tunnels of Gold

Walk along the edge of the hill to the right of the road and look down at the numerous gold diggings that dot the side of the mountain where miners followed an ancient stream bed. The gold was cemented to or deposited between the boulders that now lie strewn about the mouth of the 100-year-old mines. Some of the tunnels are a mile long, twisting and turning into the mountain. None of them are safe to explore because they have not been worked in years. The walls are crumbling, old timbers are rotted, and boulders hang ready to fall.

This area was known as Upper Bonanza Gulch by early day miners and the scar of one of the richest diggings can be seen across the valley. That operation clung to the steep side of a cliff; below it in a narrow wash are dugouts where miners lived who worked their own claims. The holes can not be seen from this point, but they can be reached by the BLM road EP 15 once you are in the valley.

From the stories told by the miners these holes, used as living quarters, were dug and first occupied by Caucasian miners who left when they thought all the gold was worked out. A number of Chinese moved in to work the skimpy leavings and they, too, lived in the dugouts. One in particular on the west bank was supposedly an opium den. The Chinese kept to themselves, bothered no one and no one bothered them—that is until word got around that their tunneling under the floor of the wash was producing plenty of gold.

The Chinese, of small stature, dug only narrow passages, just large enough to crawl in and move a short handled shovel. These miniature tunnels were useless to the White miners who talked of repossessing the wash. Rumor did seep out that the Chinese tunnels were blasted shut while the men were at work but there was no factual report as to why there were no more Chinese seen around Bonanza Gulch. In recent years prospectors have broken into small tunnels and unearthed human bones, short-handled picks and shovels.

Far to the left of the valley are other mines and an occasional building. One cabin clinging to the mountain side was the temporary home of Hatfield the rain maker. Hatfield build a dam below the cabin on a natural runoff system from Black Mountain, the predominating earthen mass to the east. Theoretically, a big rain would carry gold down from the mountain and deposit it against the dam from which it could be easily collected. Hatfield started the rain, but, as in other places, he couldn't turn it off at the right time. The dam broke and water and gold, along with Hatfield's dream, tumbled down into Bonanza Gulch where nuggets are still found.

Scenic Backcountry

If you went down into the valley with a four-wheel drive vehicle you can continue on EP 15 for 1.7 miles and you are in the main wash of Last Chance Canyon. Turn right and go 0.9 miles to the "T" and the road signs which are discussed below. Or you can return to the main road after the Bonanza Gulch side trip and turn left taking the left-most branch of two routes. The right branch goes along a rim back to the Holly Cleanser ruins. By taking the left branch there is a gradual descent for the next 1.4 miles which levels off in the main channel of Last Chance Canyon at a "T" in the road where there are numerous signs giving mileage to different locations. A half a mile back you probably saw the sign on the right indicating you were entering Red Rock Canyon State Park. This is scenic backcountry, an area favored by campers, explorers, and photographers. Since you are within the boundaries of the state park, no collecting of rocks or artifacts is allowed. There is a surprising amount of traffic, especially on weekends and road courtesy is essential. Pull off onto solid, level areas so the other visitor can pass without having to drive onto a sandy shoulder; the big campers and travel trailers especially need consideration.

At the "T" on the valley floor take the road to the right (the left branch is part of trip #9). As previously mentioned, the park rangers specifically request that only four-wheel drive vehicles, ATV's and dirt bikes enter the canyon given the extensive sandy conditions of the wash. The main road meanders along a dry creek bed between cliffs of bone-colored silica that through the ages have been sculptured into geological grandeur. Here is a chapter of earth's history telling of ancient volcanic explosions that laid down a great mantle of white silica and then capped the whole thing with a lava flow. Later the mountain range lifted toward the south and sank to the north. Erosion set to work on the soft silica, undermining and carrying it away until the rhyolite cap collapsed in jumbled masses, jagged crags, and steep cliffs, exposing islands of varied color that give the canyon its unique beauty. This is nature's studio where line, color and design is exhibited on a gigantic scale.

One and two tenths miles from the point of entering the canyon at the "T," there is an unusual formation of feldspar appearing like steps on a flat granite wall to your left. Immediately to the right of the road is one camp area that would accommodate a number of vehicles. The road curves around the granite on your left for

Unusual formation of Feldspar appears like steps along the side of a granite wall.

0.2 miles and the granite wall abruptly ends. A road to your left leads to a camp area below a natural bridge. A dozen or more vehicles can fit into this picturesque, sheltered area, where sounds echo against the mountainside and at night the stars seem almost too large and bright to be real. As previously mentioned, you need to check in with the Red Rock Canyon State Park Ranger Station if you are going to camp in the canyon. Personnel will inform you about acceptable camping locations.

Dutch Cleanser Diggings

Seven-tenths of a mile beyond the natural bridge camp area is the first of two roads turning right. The next road is 0.1 miles further. Immediately to the left of the second road is Adams Camp and Mining Company. An American flag is usually flying. Turn to the right off either of them and go 0.6 miles to reach white eroded cliffs where the remains of the Dutch Cleanser mine are located and where a petrified forest once stood. The standing trees, stumps and logs have gone home with collectors, but there are still twigs, roots and sizeable slivers of blue to brown agatized wood showing. As the silica erodes away, new pieces are exposed. Remember collecting of material is not permitted because the area is within the boundaries of Red Rock Canyon State Park.

There are level parking and camping spots near the beautiful cliffs. Old roads that were used in the days of the mining operation wind through the forest and are still fun to explore as they go over and around humps of silica. For color photography, early morning and toward evening are best. The fantastic erosion patterns in the white cliffs become nothing in the glare of mid-day sunlight. Because of the intense reflection here, this is definitely no place to be on a hot summer day! At the northern end of the valley area looking up to the top of the cliffs you can see one of the openings to the Dutch Cleanser Mine. Located in a layer of Volcanic ash, the mined material was lowered to the floor via a tram. The remains are still visible. A road leads up to the base of the tram operation and a trail leads up to the first of the tram remains and heads off to the right. It is quite a hike, even for the hardy, but the view at the top is very impressive. There are remains of equipment and several horizontal mine shafts on the ledge. You can look into the large rooms that were excavated, but it is unsafe to enter. You can see large chunks of the roof that have fallen. Even a hard hat offers no protection from one of the falling pieces. In general, the hike to the top is not recommended. However, if one must climb to the top, take plenty of water, stay on the path, be careful not to slip and stay out of the mine shafts. Such a hike should only be made in cool weather and taking a camera is a must.

Rejoining the main road after the Dutch Cleanser Mine and petrified forest side trip, there is a steep mountain with a large white stake on top 0.6 miles ahead that forces the path to go either right or left. This part of the trip should only be taken if one is interested in walking a quarter of a mile to view the old Cudahay Camp where the miners stayed and where the headquarters of the Dutch Cleanser Mine was located. The last tenth of a mile of the road is difficult when crossing the stream bed. Be careful. The mountain has extensive gold diggings along a ledge that can be seen from the road. Known as Grubstake Hill, it was worked by men who needed enough gold to replenish their supplies so they could go elsewhere to dig gold. The matrix holding the gold was so difficult to remove from the precious metal that it was mined only as a last resort.

Opal and Jasper Sightings

This is a good place to turn around or go to the right. The left arm of the road becomes too rough. Part of the old road is gone, boulders block the way and the side walls come in too close for comfort. The road on the right side of the small mountain with the white stake on top is steep, dropping down to the old Cudahay campsite. There are two Joshua trees visible on the road. Do not take this road! If you have time, a hike of a quarter-mile will bring you to the old Cudahay "Dutch Cleanser" camp site. The pumice processed here came from a ridge above the petrified forest discussed previously. You can see a number of foundations close to Salt Cedar trees and a couple of wells. Across the wash is a large mine opening. Do not enter for obvious safety reasons. The road continuing on down the canyon was used by the miners to transport the mined material to the Southern Pacific track on the Red Rock-Randsburg Road for loading and hauling to the processing mills.

The road to the right (0.6 mi.) dead ends at a camp with a dry falls to climb. Jasper, fire and milk opal may be seen. You'll cross a wash several times and it's very difficult. Again, no collecting is allowed.

The return trip to Highway 14, back tracking, will be all new. The view from this direction, the change in lighting, color and angle of the formations gives double value in spectacular scenery. It is a canyon that beckons you back time and time again, and each visit will reveal additional beauty that changes with the time of day, the season and your own awareness.

Special events such as this Valentine's Day dinner party are still held at the Opera House in Randsburg. The annual Floozy Contest was held and guests included gunfighters from the Red Rock Canyon Gang. Music was provided by Justus and the Montana's. Photo courtesy of Tom and Bobby Underwood.

The old mine tailings of the Yellow Aster Mine in Randsburg are disappearing under the encroaching tailings of the Rand Mining Company.

Photograph of the Yellow Aster Mine taken between 1903-06. The first small mill is on the left side of the canyon. A new larger mill is on the upper right side. The office building is on the right side of the road with the porch and flagpole.

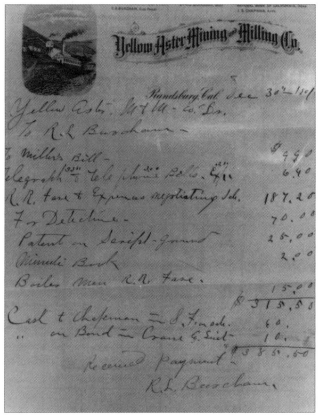

A Yellow Aster Mining and Milling Company billing statement dated December 30, 1901. It is signed by Rose La Monte Burcham, a lady doctor who was the wife of Charles Austin Burcham.

28

First load of ore from the Yellow Aster Mine being hauled to the Garlock Mill.

Early 1900s photograph of the Randsburg School.

View of the Cudahy pumice deposit that was used in Dutch Cleanser in Last Chance Canyon. The remains of the old tram works are visible in the center of the picture. The mine shafts were located along the white volcanic ash layer almost at the top of the mountain.

Along the high volcanic ash ledge are the equipment remains of the top part of the tram. Also visible is one of the horizontal shafts used in the mining of the pumice.

View of one of the spectacular rock formations in Red Rock Canyon.

The Desert Tortoise Discovery Center is open during the spring along the Randsburg-Mojave Road.

Old photograph of the Cudahy mining operation in Last Chance Canyon. Pumice for Dutch Cleanser came from the ledge of white, top left. Track for ore cars bringing material to the valley floor is the long sweeping line down through the center of the picture.

Chinese miners relaxed with their pipe, a bit of gambling or a few drinks in this dugout in Upper Bonanza Gulch near the entrance to Last Chance Canyon.

Remains of a house dug out of solid rock by a World War I veteran is still used today by weekend campers in the Summit Diggings area.

View of a Southern Pacific train exiting a tunnel built in 1908 in the Summit Diggings area.

Moving shadows and changing light give the Pinnacles an air of fantasy.

In spring, this Pinnacle formation is surrounded by a carpet of wildflowers.

In the spring near the El Paso Mountains flocks of sheep graze the desert as a lone Basque herder and his dog guide and guard them.

Openings to mine tunnels, dynamite storage caves and prospect test holes pockmark the desert as the Randsburg-Mojave Road nears Highway 395.

A 1923 photograph of miners homes in back of the Kelly Silver Mine in
Red Mountain. A water line runs across the front of the photograph.

The Kelly Silver Mine at the south edge of Red Mountain. The photograph
was taken between 1915 and 1920. Silver ore was so rich here that men rode
shotgun on the wagons that hauled it the few feet from the mine to the mill.

Atolia around World War I when the community was thriving during the tungsten mining boom.

The stage arrives somewhere between Garlock and Goler in the late 1890s.

Headframe of the old Union Mine on the dirt road going from the Randsburg-Mojave Road to Atolia.

Ruins of the Barker Mill easily viewed from Highway 395 south of Red Mountain.

Holes in the earth that were once the hub of the Buckboard Mine in the Stringer Mining District.

A vertical mine shaft near the Buckboard Mine. This is one of many in the Stringer Mining District.

The old Windy Mine just outside of Randsburg.

A-frames, loading chutes, mine dumps, abandoned mill buildings and rusted metal encroach upon the tiny community of Red Mountain.

Garlock residents in 1896 have a Sunday picnic up at the Narrows in Goler Canyon.

Early 1900s photograph of the Goler pumping station.

Wildflowers on Kohen Dry Lake — looking towards the El Paso Mountains.

Wildflowers in the El Paso Mountains.

Red Rock Canyon, Neuralia Road, and Randsburg-Mojave Road

From a land of fantasy that grips the imagination to miles of peaceful solitude, this is an area to visit during the cool months between October and June.

ravelers on Highway 14, heading north from Mojave, cut through Red Rock Canyon and have only a mini look at a few colorful cliffs before the road returns to stretches of sand, sage, mesquite and Joshua. The limited view from a speeding car isn't even a sample of what can be enjoyed by taking a few of the side roads. Behind the cliffs, around a corner or over a hump is unique beauty in color and shape. The good dirt trails are short exploratory trips to exceptional views and eroded formations. Be sure to stop in at the Red Rock Canyon State Park Ranger Station 4 miles north of the junction of Highway 14 and the Red Rock-Randsburg Road. If you are going north on Highway 14 turn left on Abbott road. The ranger station, visitor center and Ricardo campground is 0.7 miles in the park on a paved road. If you are going south on Highway 14 turn right on Abbott Road. The visitor center is located in the old town site of Ricardo; the rangers are happy to answer questions you may have about the area. There is an excellent campground at this location. Red Rock Canyon is within the boundaries of the State Park which was created in 1968.

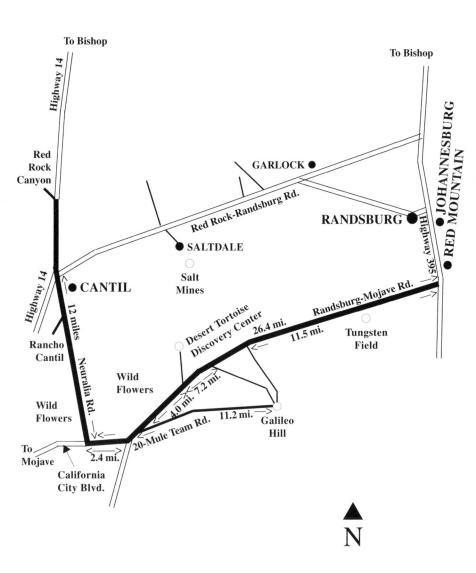

**RED ROCK CANYON, NEURALIA ROAD,
AND RANDSBURG-MOJAVE ROAD**

Over the years, the park has expanded from its original 4,000 acres to its present 10,000 acres.

Nature's Sculpture

Through the years, visitors in their fertile imagination have given names to the wonders of nature's sculpture. There is Cathedral City, the White House Cliffs, Buried City, Heliopolis Temple of the Sun, Tai Shan Temple and such mundane things as Camel Rocks and Elephant Head. Much of Red Rock's back country has appeared in movie and T.V. shows and they have called the formations hideouts, outlaw country, and spy headquarters. No two people see the same thing in this wonderland.

Find a high spot and gaze down upon this enigma of color, cliffs, valleys and roads where a hundred years ago only a wagon trail wound in and out of the boulders in the main wash. There were few early travelers, except for Remi Nadeau's teams. Silver from Cerro Gordo, Owens Lake country, was hauled over this route to the Los Angeles market. Some place in Red Rock Canyon was a way station where there was food for men and animals, a place to change teams, rest and exchange the latest news from north and south.

The canyon was beautiful then as now, but many of those early day freighters left the impression that they dreaded the drive through the deep sand that pulled at the wagon wheels until the horses and mules were unable to keep the load moving. The load south was only one layer of silver ingots on the wagon bed but they were heavy. The return trip brought hay stacked high and a perfect wind catcher.

Wind and sand were bad enough but rain was the real threat. Beautiful thunderheads along the canyon rim was a warning that no time should be lost in getting out to the open desert. Flash floods moved everything in their path tumbling boulders, wagons, teams and drivers. One driver lived to tell of his jump from the wagon and desperate scramble up a hillside. The load of silver, wagon and team was buried somewhere under tons of debris. Fifty years later a silver ingot found in the canyon was believed to have been from this incident. Speaking of flash floods, you can see the results of the major flash flood in the summer of 1997 as you look to the south at the entrance of Red Rock Canyon.

Treasures for the Assayer or Artist

The canyon has much to offer any visitor. You can let your imagination contemplate finding a treasure of at least one load of silver bullion still buried in the canyon or along one of its drainage channels. The photographer and artist will find another type of treasure in the elusive beauty that challenges man and modern techniques. The railroad buff can trace out the Red Rock Railroad line that was washed out by an old flash flood that left rails twisted like pretzels.

The test of any adventure lies not only in the canyon but along the roads radiating out and beyond its pageant of grandeur. Four miles south of the Red Rock Canyon Ranger Station where Highway 14 intersects the Red Rock-Randsburg Road, turn left and immediately turn right taking Neuralia Road going south. After crossing the railroad track a cluster of houses on the right is an example of present day determination to carve out a home in the desert. The small settlement is Rancho Seco. It was built by a group of retirees and weekenders who fought wind, sand and flood to make their plans reality.

Driving 2.6 miles south on Neuralia Road is the Honda Proving Center of California. Located on the left hand side of the road, Honda turned an old ranch into a major North American vehicle testing center. From the north as you approach the facility you can see the outline of the testing track.

A Shimmering Sea

Neuralia Road leaves the old ranch country and cuts through desert that can be on the move when the wind is at work, a shimmering sea of heat waves in summer or a garden of wildflowers in spring. Like a carpet of green and purple, acres of Persian Prince or Thistle Sage spread out to a lavender haze in the distance. A close examination of the plant that stands approximately two feet high reveals one of the desert's most fascinating wild flowers. A series of flower clusters like pale green balls of wool encircled with lacy orchid blooms are supported on a stout purplish stem covered with white wool. Acres of these unusual flowers stand above the less conspicuous Frost Mat, a rosette of minute green leaves and white flowers that hug the ground. A few poppies, and other blooms of gold add an interesting color contrast. The amount of flowers in any area depends upon the amount and timing of rain during the winter and spring.

When Neuralia Road enters California City, turn left onto California City Blvd. This is a place to replenish supplies and check the gas tank because there are no gas stations in the Randsburg area. In California City, there are gas stations, restaurants and hotel accommodations. The town has golf courses and is a center for glider flights. The airport is on the west side of town off California City Blvd.

Stay on California City Blvd. 2.4 miles to the intersection of California City Blvd. and the Randsburg-Mojave Road. A golf course is on the left side of the road. Turn left onto the Randsburg -Mojave Road and go 1.3 miles to a "Y" in the road. In the center of the "Y" is a covered picnic area with a bulletin board telling the story of the desert tortoise and its habitat. The dirt road to the left is the old Randsburg-Mojave wagon road going straight into Highway 395 and the Rand mining area. The road to the right is paved and is called 20 Mule Team Road. It goes to the Silver Saddle Ranch Resort and Galileo Peak which is 11.2 miles further on the paved road.

Turtle Territory

Obviously at this point a choice must be made. Four miles further on the Randsburg-Mojave dirt road is the Desert Tortoise Preserve and Discovery Center where visitors can observe desert tortoises in their natural habitat. During the months of March - May the preserve is staffed with a naturalist. Cooler months of the year is the time to observe desert tortoise activity during daylight hours.

If you go to the Desert Tortoise Preserve, you can also go to Galileo Peak which is an excellent observation point for the whole area. If you go to Galileo Peak directly, you will miss the Desert Tortoise Preserve.

Let's assume you decide to take the Randsburg-Mojave Road and go to the Desert Tortoise Preserve first. Ahead are the great open spaces along a route traveled 100 years ago by ore wagons, stage coaches and spring wagons used by people hauling their gold to Mojave, meeting the train, replenishing supplies or on their way out to "civilization." Those early travelers had little choice of vehicle or weather conditions. Today the trip is made in comfort, and visitors can select the time of year.

Spring is the most ideal time to drive this old wagon road that encourages frequent stops just for viewing the land, and inhaling the pot-pourri fragrance of wild flowers. It is an easy place to relax for the sight of gently swaying plants that send ripples of yellow, white and lavender toward the distant horizon have a hypnotic effect that shuts out a frenzied world. The display varies from year to year depending on rainfall and temperatures, but from early March to mid-May chances are good that fiddleneck, desert candle, poppy, coreopsis, gilias, yellow saucers, blazing stars and many others will greet the visitor.

Four miles from the "Y" on the Randsburg-Mojave Road is the entrance to the Desert Tortoise Preserve. Turn left and go straight 0.6 miles to the parking area. From March-May a motor home is parked with a naturalist in attendance who is there to answer questions that visitors may have. The Desert Tortoise Preserve is a large and growing privately owned fenced area. The Desert Tortoise Preserve Committee located in Riverside, California is responsible for creating this preserve and also undertaking a number of other projects whose purpose is to rebuild the desert tortoise population in this and other areas of Southern California.

The preserve has a number of well marked trails for visitors to explore. If you are there during the time the naturalist is in attendance (March-May) you will be able to pick up a number of publications about the preserve, the area, and the committee's role in the preservation of the desert tortoise.

Silver Saddle Oasis

When you are finished exploring this area, go back to the main road, turn left, and continue on the Randsburg-Mojave Road another 7.2 miles. On your left will appear a large tan California City water tank. And immediately on your right is a dirt road to the Silver Saddle Ranch Resort and Galileo Peak. If you want to take this side trip, turn right on this dirt road and go 0.3 miles. Turn right again and go 1.0 miles where the dirt road becomes paved at the intersection of Santa Clara and Rutgers Road. Continue on the paved road which is now Rutgers 0.9 miles to the intersection with Kennedy Road. Turn left on this excellent paved road 0.8 miles to the entrance of the Silver Saddle Ranch Resort. The resort is a beautiful oasis in the desert. Although this facility is a membership resort, the restaurant is open to the public for breakfast, lunch and dinner. Also, camping is permitted for a fee and there are a few RV hookups for the public. To get to Galileo Peak, continue on this well-maintained road as it winds up to a peak that offers a spectacular view of the surrounding desert. You will have to stop at the picnic area two-thirds of the way up the hill and walk the rest of the way. Take plenty of water and remember that this is a good hike in cool weather. Ancient roads, new roads, and miles of desert are seen as if from a plane. The San Bernardino Mountains on one side and the Sierras on the other seem so close. Even Telescope Peak of Death Valley, over 150 miles away, shows its snow-covered peak against dark blue sky.

When you are finished with this side trip, retrace your steps back to the water tank and the Randsburg-Mojave Road. Turn right where the Randsburg-Mojave Road continues through a wide flat valley that, in spring, is the feeding grounds of large flocks of sheep. The sight and sounds of hundreds of ewes and their lambs conversing and eating, while a lone man and his dog guide and guard, is a scene of pastoral life similar to that in many European countries. The herder, a Basque, was raised in a land between Spain and France where his skills were learned as a small boy, alone on a mountainside, watching the family flock.

Characteristic of the desert are miles that show little of man's scars but suddenly deep gouges and old buildings indicate his handiwork. Heaps of mine tailings announce a tungsten field that boomed and then died when World War I needs were over.

As you approach Highway 395, to the left there is a cluster of old mine structures, tailings, and houses known as "Dog Patch." Why such a name? Who knows. Many different versions have been given and all of them (or none) may have some basis of truth. That, too, is characteristic of desert country. At this point, the Randsburg-Mojave Road turns into Osdick Road which intersects with Highway 395. Turn left onto Highway 395 and the town of Johannesburg is 2.2 miles to the north. The turnoff to Randsburg is 1.3 miles further.

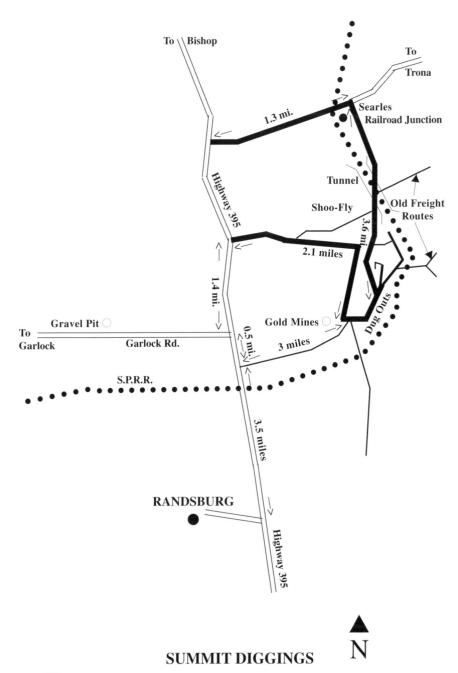

SUMMIT DIGGINGS

N

Summit Diggings

A maze of roads, placer gold diggings, dugouts, and remains of an old railroad shoo-fly, best visited in cool weather, calls for experienced desert driving.

Some adventurers climb mountains because they are there. Others enjoy following roads to see where they go. Summit Diggings is great for the road enthusiast as there are enough trails to provide exploring over a number of weekends and all within a few miles of a highway. Although this was primarily a gold mining area, not all roads were the result of mine operations. There is an old freight route for historians and artifact collectors plus camp sites and construction roads for the railroad buff.

Summit is a pie-shaped bit of desert bounded on two sides by hard-surfaced highways and by the Southern Pacific Railroad (now Union Pacific following the merger) on the other. Three miles from the highway is the heart of gold country. In the early 1890s the area was crawling with prospectors, and anyone who worked at all got some gold. Some were lucky and hit pockets of nuggets, some produced hardly enough to keep them in beans, bacon and tobacco, while still others restlessly moved about hoping to find a better location and produced nothing at all.

There are two ways to enter Summit depending on the vehicle used.

Low-Clearance Vehicle Entrance

From the intersection of the Randsburg cutoff and Highway 395 go north 3.5 miles. Just past the railroad tracks is an excellent dirt road to the right marked by a white barrel with an arrow and a sign reading "Loma-Dusenburg." This road east for 2.0 miles travels through gold camps that are still active. At the 2.0 mile point there is a "Y," keep to the right. Within 0.1 miles the road crosses the railroad tracks. Stay on the right side of the railroad tracks for another 0.7 miles, then cross the tracks again. Go down the hill 0.1 miles to BLM road RM 15. Follow RM 15 for another 0.1 miles past a "Y" where it goes to the right.

To the left a lone fireplace chimney remains from a home that burned some years ago. This is a good landmark and place to park for a look around. The fork to the left of the chimney goes through gold diggings that are still being worked and merges with the road you used to enter the area. A short drive or walk to the diggings gives one a view of the immense amount of pick and shovel work that went into the process of securing gold. This was called "dry diggings" because there was no water and the material was put through a dry washer to shake away the dirt and gravel to leave nuggets and fine gold on the riffle board.

High-Clearance Vehicle Entrance

The second road entrance is for high clearance vehicles only and will provide a view of more of the gold country. The easiest way to locate this road is to look for the dirt road to the right, heading east off Highway 395, at the white sign for a mine reading "O.C. .49," which is visible as you approach the top of the long hill 5.4 miles north of the Randsburg cutoff at Highway 395. Keep to the well-used road; lesser used routes wander back into the main road but are usually rougher, sandy or both. They are for exploring only after visitors become familiar with the lay of the land. Go 0.4 miles to a "Y," stay to the left. In 0.2 miles at another "Y," stay to the right. Go another 1.5 miles to a distinct crossroad that is 2.1 miles from the entrance on Highway 395.

At one time, one of the main roads in the area had so much use that the Automobile Club of Southern California posted their blue and white enamel signs at every cross road. They disappeared long ago as a result of gun fire and other vandalism. Those signs would still be helpful, as reassurance, because being only a short distance from the highway, one gets the feeling of being miles away from everything. It is a satisfying bit of desert for those who like to get away from the crowd. If you would be more comfortable knowing other visitors are nearby, be assured that there are bike riders just over the hill, campers tucked away behind a shielding bank, some hobby miners working their gold claims and from any high point, look west and traffic on Highway 395 is clearly visible.

The road takes broad curves and gradually descends to wind through almost colorless and sparsely vegetated hills. Here and there an outcrop of green decomposed basalt catches the eye, a bright color in contrast to the rest of the hills. To the unpracticed eye it would seem that a hill so green would have mineral wealth of some kind, but to the old time miners it was classed as "pure junkite." You pass a number of mining sites as you make your decent through a small canyon.

The lone fireplace chimney, remains from a home that burned some years ago, is a good landmark and place to park for a look around. The fork to the right of the chimney goes through gold diggings that are still being worked. A short drive or walk to the diggings gives one a view of the immense amount of pick and shovel work that went into the process of securing gold. This was called "dry diggings" because there was no water and the material was put through a dry washer to shake away the dirt and gravel to leave nuggets and fine gold on the riffle board.

Take the right-angled road for three miles and you will be back to Highway 395 without seeing anything much except placer diggings, tailings and the rock outline of old tent home sites.

For real exploring, skip the branch to the right and continue straight ahead a few more feet toward the railroad tracks to a "Y." Here the *low clearance route* joins the **high clearance route**.

Save the road that goes to the railroad for another trip. It goes under the tracks via a huge culvert and comes out into a small gold field where the clay matrix was like cement making the extraction of gold a difficult and expensive process. The road wanders through sage and greasewood to eventually emerge on a hard surfaced road near Red Mountain. In the years when rains are adequate, wildflowers carpet much of the washes and hillsides, but other than that there is little of interest.

For those taking the *high-clearance vehicle* route, stay on the left branch at the "Y" and follow BLM route RM 15 for 0.2 miles between the railroad tracks and a steep bank pitted with dugouts. For those with *low-clearance vehicles* take the right branch of the "Y" which follows BLM route RM 15 for 0.2 miles to the dugouts. Both approach routes now merge.

Tunes on a Train Whistle

A few years ago a mining company bulldozed back into this hillside and eliminated many of the dugouts which in the old days were a long row of openings that were living quarters for the miners and some families. They were in use as late as 1908-1912 when the railroad was built. One old timer recalled that as a small boy he traveled the "cushions" between Goler where his father was drilling a well and his mother was at home near Brown. When the train reached the Summit dugouts it stopped if there was anyone getting on or off or there were grocery orders to unload. Heads would pop out of the dugouts to see who was arriving, or to wave at the engineer while children streaked across the wash and up the steep embankment to pick up the supplies being dropped. One of the engineers brightened the miners' day by 'quilling' as soon as he hit the area. The tunes he played on the old steam locomotive's whistle were not always identifiable, but they were a beautiful sound floating out across the silent desert. The days he made the run were special ones for the people of the Summit. Today, you can still see weekenders working the tailings with their drywashers.

After a look around, continue on RM 15 for another 0.2 miles where RM 15 goes to the left across the wash and up a hill. At this point turn right and go 0.1 miles toward the railroad tracks. Turn left onto the road that parallels the tracks and follow this road for 0.4 miles going up a hill. To the left is a mine on the hill directly across the wash marked by the white posts. This was the first uranium discovery in the area that showed strong enough indications to warrant further exploration. That this is not uranium country is evident from the limited amount of tailings.

This spot provides a good look at the mountains stretching off to the south and west. For the railroad buffs there is also a view of the steep grade that was a nightmare to the railroad construction engineers back in 1908. Here, too, is a place where "curve grease" was frequently used.

People lived in the dugouts that line a cliff facing the railroad. Waving passengers and a delivery of groceries dropped off by the passing train were the highlights of the day.

Continue on this road for another 0.2 miles. To the left is a dugout against the hill. If someone hasn't already moved in, this is an ideal camping spot. For those in a *low-clearance vehicle* you need to stop here and walk to the dugout. The *high-clearance vehicle* can cross the wash ahead and go a short distance to the first road to the left which goes up to the level area in front of the dugout.

Home of Solid Rock

Shortly after World War I a veteran and his army nurse wife moved here where he had mine claims. In his spare time from mining and hauling water, the disabled veteran carved a home out of solid rock. Few early day desert homes were as cool in summer or as warm in winter. A generator provided lights and power for a radio, but it was still a lonely existence for the wife who was city raised. Sometimes the gold ran thin and the veteran's disability check was so small that they would be on the verge of starvation. Other times the gold provided gas for the generator, food, kept the old car running and gave them a night of celebrating in the then wide open town of Red Mountain.

From this point, *low-clearance vehicle* explorers need to hike, *high-clearance vehicles* may continue on the road paralleling the railroad tracks for 0.4 miles to view the railroad tunnel that was built by Southern Pacific in 1908. The road crosses three washes to get to the tunnel which is unique in having the date stamped at the top of the opening. The tunnel was the longest in Southern Pacific history at that time, being 4,340 feet long. There are several old telegraph and later telephone poles still standing. Late in the afternoon the train goes through the tunnel to pick up cars dropped off by the Trona Railroad.

Now is the time to backtrack past the dugout where the veteran lived, past the uranium mine for another 0.4 miles to the road that you came down to the railroad tracks. Turn right and go 0.1 miles and you are back on RM 15. *Low-clearance vehicles* will have to backtrack to Highway 395; go back past the first dugouts and follow the route out that was discussed in the first part of the chapter under "Entrance for Low Clearance Vehicles."

For *high-clearance vehicles* stay on RM 15 crossing the wash and go 0.9 miles. RM 15 turns left, but stay on the road that is going up the mountain. Another 0.1 miles brings you to an old railroad bed that was part of a shoo-fly, the temporary tracks to get the train over El Paso Summit until a tunnel could be built. Cross this "T," which not only has the railroad bed but also a road, and continue on between two showy strawberry pink hills. Up a slight incline for another 0.6 miles the road crosses the second part of the old shoo-fly railroad bed.

Shoo-Fly Operation

The shoo-fly made a roundabout trip along the mountainside and eventually got over the top. It took many engines as helpers and an unusual "Y" for them to reverse direction and return to the lower level ready to boost the next train over the top.

You can drive on the old shoo-fly a short distance on either side of the road, but areas are caving off. The best route is to go ahead approximately 0.3 miles, making a sharp turn to the right and you will be on the roadbed which goes through a cut and back to where you first crossed it. The sides are sloughing off in places and it may not be wide enough to travel for many more years, but it is no great distance to walk. Up on the level to the east of the old roadbed are signs of a construction camp or blacksmith shop. A search would undoubtedly turn up collectibles such as four inch diameter washers, with patent date May-10-04, found half-embedded in the loose dirt. It takes days to follow all the old construction roads, but along them are the temporary camp sites and discards of bottles, tins and metal scrap.

Above the shoo-fly is a "Y": the right branches off into an old freight road that edged around Searles Lake and headed for the Panamint mine camps. It stretches out across the desert with overnight camp sites about every ten miles. The ruts cut by the heavy wagons are a scar that has remained through the years and will for many more generations. The camp sites are usually recognizable by the sparse vegetation where the horses and mules grazed, rolled and stomped through the nights, and by the scattered broken glass, old liquor bottles, rusted condensed milk cans and wide-mouthed sardine tins. Most of the old trail is not for passenger car travel.

If you take the left arm of the "Y" there will be a barbed wire fence and old telegraph poles 0.6 miles from the second part of the shoo-fly you crossed which indicates where the railroad tunnel surfaces. The right branch following down the fence travels toward the line of loaded and empty freight cars for 1.1 miles. You may witness the Trona train pulling in with its load of chemicals or Southern Pacific engines busy switching cars in preparation of the haul out to Mojave. Chances are you will see the train going through the Summit or the tunnel but no one will quill you a tune for now. The old steam locomotive, the prospectors and the creaking freight wagons are but a memory.

Down near the switching area is the hard-surfaced road that goes north to Trona or left 1.3 miles to dead end into Highway 395. Turn left and go approximately 6.8 miles and you are back at the Randsburg cutoff. A day or a weekend, the route has covered approximately 20 miles, and leaves a multitude of beckoning roads for many more days of exploring.

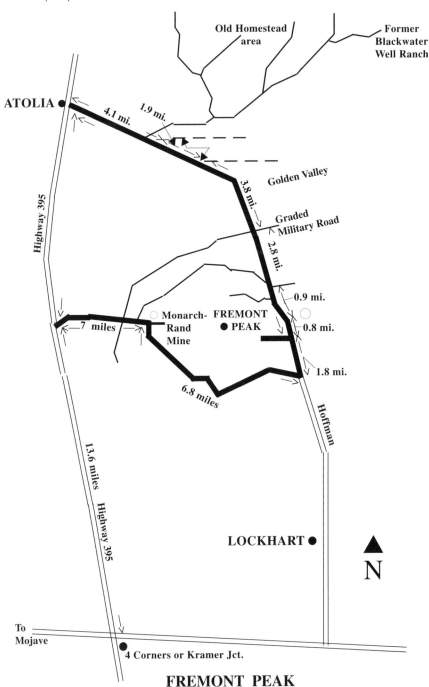

Old Homestead area

Former Blackwater Well Ranch

ATOLIA

4.1 mi.

1.9 mi.

Golden Valley

3.8 mi.

Graded Military Road

Highway 395

2.8 mi.

0.9 mi.

Monarch-Rand Mine

FREMONT PEAK

0.8 mi.

7 miles

1.8 mi.

6.8 miles

Hoffman

13.6 miles Highway 395

LOCKHART

N

To Mojave

4 Corners or Kramer Jct.

FREMONT PEAK

Loop Trip Around Fremont Peak

From October to June this virtually undisturbed region is ideal for relaxing, getting acquainted with the land, the native plants and animals, and oneself. Plan a leisurely visit. This trip <u>requires</u> the use of a truck or four-wheel drive vehicle.

remont Peak country has little scenery that would be classed as "spectacular," but it does provide for a variety of interests and a wealth that lies in values for the restoration of man's well-being. Rare in today's world of Southern California are two ingredients that abound in the peak area—space and quiet. There is little to interfere with the slight sound of displaced gravel as a lizard darts for cover. Audible, too, is the soft swish of limber branches as greasewoods sway and bow to a passing breeze.

Overhead the desert raven and an occasional eagle circle and glide high and effortlessly on their own private air stream. Within reach, a Saw-Whet Owl humped on a Joshua limb pretends that no one is around, while sparrow, vireo, thrasher, or flycatcher cross and recross the trail in the daily business of acquiring food. It is a place of tranquility most of the time.

Fremont Peak itself rises steeply 4,584 feet above the floor of Golden Valley. The valley is believed to have received its name from the golden glow that appears at sunset. The peak, a landmark used by early travelers and the 20-mule team borax wagon men, was named for John C. Fremont during the 1850s when his popularity was running high. His name marked not only outstanding peaks but graced canyons, counties, and towns in over a hundred different places. One by one the name was changed to that of a local hero or a more favored identification. By 1900 Fremont Peak and a railroad siding opposite it along the Randsburg Railroad were the only legally recognized places still carrying the Fremont name in all of California. Gradually the name is reappearing along the route of his early travels.

Today the peak that can be seen for miles stands rugged and rocky-sided, inviting and challenging those who like to climb mountains, explore in search of little known plant life, untouched rock and mineral deposits or the haunts of small wildlife.

Twenty-two miles north of the junction of State Highway 58 and U.S. Highway 395, at Four Corners (or Kramer Junction), is the little mining settlement of Atolia. At the north end of the cluster of buildings just past the blue call box #395-692 (which is 23.1 miles north of Four Corners) take the well-graded dirt road to the right heading east.

If you are traveling south on Highway 395 from Randsburg and are at the intersection of the Randsburg-Red Rock Road and Highway 395, turn right and go south for 8.3 miles. At the north end of the town of Atolia just before the blue call box #395-692 the well-graded dirt road is clearly visible to the left. Turn left onto this dirt road. At this point, Red Mountain is on the left and Fremont Peak is off in the distance to the southeast.

Old structures that played an important part in the process of mining stand silent, sun dried and wind carved, monuments to a past of wealth.

Tons of Tungsten

Take this well-graded dirt road going east for 0.4 miles and turn right onto the dirt road that is heading south. Follow this road for 0.4 miles to the large wooden headframe (large wooden mining structure). The headframe is clearly visible as soon as you turn onto the dirt road from Highway 395. As you go towards the headframe, you can see tungsten mines, dumps and abandoned headframes, some of which date back to World War I. This is private property and one should not leave the road without permission of the mining company at Atolia. Actually there is little need to leave the road. The colorful tailing piles, aged wood frames and mine pits are as interesting and photographically challenging viewed from the traveled path as they would be from any other point.

From the headframe follow the dirt road around it. Just past the headframe, you come to a "Y." The right branch goes into a fenced area. Take the left branch for 0.1 miles and turn left. You will again be going east on a wide, old graded road. This was a main route east that has not been used for many years, nature is recapturing its own. Rains have left their mark, but the road is still passable. Follow this road east along the old power lines for 0.6 miles to another "Y" with water tanks on the right. At the "Y," take the right branch following the old graded road for another 1.9 miles. The old road gets very rough; a newer road to the left with fewer rocks, parallels the old graded road.

After going in an easterly direction and down this gradual valley descent for the 1.9 miles, another "Y" appears. Do not take the left branch; the right branch is a good dirt road that goes in a southeasterly direction towards Fremont Peak. Three-tenths of a mile before this last "Y" you will have passed on your right an interesting below-ground cement tank complex that is heavily fenced.

Cowboy Patrol

On the first part of this trip, the roads to the left branch out to old homestead plots, mining projects and eventually end up at the old Blackwater Ranch or against the Navy reservation at the side of the ranch. Most of the area was private property, patrolled by cowboys who not only herded cattle but also kept pumps running at a number of watering places. The dim trails follow old line fences, and end up at former homestead sites, recognized by rusted metal, twisted fencing, metal sheeting so bullet riddled that it gives the appearance of having gone through a great battle, and sandblasted old posts leaning away from the wind.

The route to Fremont Peak travels a section of the old cattle country, too, and in spring the carpet of green gives credence to its former use as range land, but in winter there is a bareness that belies this use. Tepee-shaped bunches of dry, course grass are hardly noticeable to the inexperienced eye, yet they dot the valley and are rich in nutrition as cattle feed. In the first edition of this book it was said "If the fence gates are up, close them behind you." But now all is abandoned, and your trip will take you past two former gate and fence line complexes.

Stay on the well-used road heading for the peak, ignoring cross-roads that are graded for use by army, air force or power line maintenance. Creosote bushes grow close to the road and, like a welcoming committee, will reach in an open car window or slide along an unsuspecting arm resting on the window ledge. This is an old route called Hoffman Road that was used by wagons many yesterdays ago; there was no need for a wide path then as there is no need for one today.

Along the good dirt road heading for Fremont Peak, within 0.4 miles you'll cross two washes. In another 0.2 miles an old road crosses a good road that is being traveled. Don't take either branch but keep going straight. Within another 0.1 mile or 4.1 miles from Highway 395, the first of two old gates and barbed wire fence lines is crossed.

Stay to the Left

Eight-tenths of a mile further or 4.9 miles from Highway 395 there is an intersection with a major dirt road. The left branch goes to Cuddeback Dry Lake and the right branch goes back to Highway 395. Don't take either the right or left branch. Within another 0.4 miles another old dirt road is intersected. To the left, an old water tank and well are visible. Continuing on the good dirt road in a southeasterly direction for another 0.7 miles, the second gate and barbed-wire fence line is crossed. Again, don't take any roads to the right as you travel through this area, but keep going straight.

After another 1.4 miles or 7.4 miles from Highway 395, the

top of a knoll is reached with a good view of the Cuddeback Dry Lake depression on the left. Straight ahead the road that will be traveled can be seen going down into and through the depression and then back up an incline between volcanic hills on the left and Fremont Peak on the right. Do not take the dirt road that goes to the right on the top of this knoll. This is a good place to get out and walk around for the view. There are signs that people camp in this area.

Continue on another 2.3 miles or 9.8 miles from Highway 395, two major dirt roads intersect at the bottom of the Cuddeback Dry Lake depression which are crossed. The second intersection 0.1 mile after the first has the left branch with the BLM road marker EF 473 going to Cuddeback Lake. The right branch goes up the grade to the west side of Fremont Peak and back to Highway 395. Do not take any roads going left or right, but keep going straight. Just after this major intersection, the BLM road marker EF 454 which is the BLM name for the old Hoffman Road appears.

Continuing on Hoffman Road and EF 454 in a southeasterly direction for another 2 miles or 11.8 miles from Highway 395 the foot of Fremont Peak is reached which is on the right. A small playa is on the right with a road on the right going to the dry basin. From this point the road follows the contour of the mountain on the southeast side. Hoffman Road (EF 454) goes between the peak, on the right, and colorful volcanic hills, on the left. Eight-tenths of a mile past the northern end of the startlingly smooth, cream colored playa at the base of Fremont Peak or 12.6 miles from Highway 395, a road to the left takes a short one mile side trip into these hills. The road into the hills grows narrow and faint past the one mile point. Anything other than four-wheel drive vehicles should not attempt any part of this side trip. The point of interest is one mile into the hills. The road continues on to an abandoned mineral prospect.

Pastel Ambiance

At the one-mile point there is a sheltered spot to camp and unique geological contrasts to explore. On one side is pastel colored, chalk-like material. The yellow is sinter deposited out of an ancient steam vent, the gray is diorite, a blend of granite and banded rhyolite. The opposite side of the road is steep, rough and a composition of dark volcanic rock where flesh-colored feldspar is just starting to erode out to the surface. There is a definite indication of a pegmetite dyke, quartz crystals forming and some hornblende crystals. A search should turn up garnet. There are more hills to explore and a bit of digging could uncover a virgin field for crystal and mineral collectors.

Here is an ideal place for beginning geologists or student field trips, for within this small area is visual evidence of recent volcanic action, steam vent deposits, cinder cone rhyolite, older igneous intrusions and every form of quartz. A fine example of an alluvial fan comes down from Fremont Peak to a playa of clay that is hard and smooth when dry, soft and sticky when wet.

Other roads branch off into the pink and tan hills for those who wish to explore the geological wonders. Within 0.9 miles of the first described side trip, or 13.5 miles from Highway 395, there is a distinct "Y" at the northern end of a second and larger playa. The right branch goes directly across the playa for 0.5 miles. This route misses the mill site and should not be attempted except in very dry weather conditions when the playa is dried out. The left branch will curve to the left around the large playa for 0.4 miles to a mill site. Older placer diggings and remains of the Hamburger Mill border the lake. For the relic collector there are interesting shapes in rusted iron, for the antique car enthusiast there are rusted fenders and car parts dating back to the 1920s, and somewhere within walking distance should be the cook house dump for a bottle collector's dig. Photographers will find the ruins, the prospect holes, and the cracked pattern of the dried silt, interesting subject matter.

Wild Gardens

When there have been winter rains, the narrow cuts, between the hills and the valley, between Fremont Peak and the volcanic area, become wild flower gardens with a wide variety of plants. Though desert climate conditions are severe, plant life has developed devices for continued existence and some bloom each year regardless of the lack of moisture. Most have protective coats on their seeds so that there will be no germination until conditions are just right, regardless of the years of waiting. Variations in the spring display is not only influenced by moisture, but also by the elevation and soil conditions. What will grown at one elevation does not appear at other heights and practically none will survive out of their natural habitat. For the naturalist this area has much of interest. There are still unidentified plants to be discovered and hundreds of mini-flowers that have drawn little or no attention though they are extremely beautiful when viewed through a magnifying glass.

As previously mentioned, the road skirts the left side of the dry basin 0.4 miles to the mill site. After visiting the mill site, the mill road goes back to the main road for 0.5 miles and connects with the main road at the southern end. This connecting road is 0.6 miles from the northern end of the playa if one stayed on Hoffman Road and skipped the visit to the mill site. At some points it may be difficult to see the road as a result of a confusion of motorcycle tracks. It is easily picked up again on the south side of the dry basin and Hoffman Road or EF 454 continues in a south-easterly direction. Within 0.2 miles from the southern end of the playa or 14.3 miles from Highway 395, a side road to the right goes into a sheltered cove that is a delightful camping spot. Camping on the east side of Fremont Peak, the sheltered side because the prevailing winds are out of the northwest, is a do-it-yourself proposition with only level spots developed by nature. Food, water, fuel and

Relic of the Hamburger Mill on the edge of a playa along Hoffman Road.

shelter must be carried in and refuse carried out.

From this particular cove there is a view of a long valley reaching to the horizon and the distant settlements of Lockhart and Hinkley, where the old road terminated for travelers coming this way before the turn of the century. No doubt they, too, found this a pleasant place to camp and enjoyed the same kind of wonderful nights that seemingly bring the large and bright stars almost within touching distance in the immense sky. With no highrises to shut out or distort, the wonder of the earth's movement can be witnessed as the full moon appears at the edge of the horizon. The moon, like the stars, seems so large with its light so bright.

Little Night Folk

If there is no conversation or human movement, the little night people with bright eyes, sensitive whiskers and long tails will start to move about. In time they will move close, tempted by the smell of crumbs or water and their antics will provide hours of unusual entertainment.

A mile and eight-tenths from the camp site, or 2 miles from the southern part of the dry playa, or 16.1 miles from Atolia and Highway 395, the main road branches at the eastern most part of Fremont Peak. Take the road to the right. A BLM road sign says "EF 411" and goes to the right. The left branch is the continuation of the Hoffman Road and EF 454 that goes to Lockhart and in approximately eighteen miles reaches State Highway 58.

The route to the right (EF 411) continues up a grade along the

Remains of the Monarch-Rand Mine on the west side of Fremont Peak.

southern foothills of Fremont Peak. The next 6.8 miles follows the contour of the mountain going in a southern direction first and then at the south side of Fremont Peak the road goes west. Within

3.4 miles from where EF 411 turns right, there is a dirt road to the right going up into the mountain where it dead ends. Vegetation changes as does the terrain. Reefs of slate, like the humps and spines of some prehistoric animal, curve along the high ridges, entirely different than the opposite side of the peak.

Six and eight-tenths miles from the turnoff onto EF 411 a road going to the right has another BLM sign marked EF 411. The road branching left misses the trip to the Monarch-Rand Mine and goes to Highway 395. The good road to the right goes a mile to the ruins of the old mine, once an active camp built around a rich gold and tungsten strike. The remains indicate how extensive the operation had been with a mill, settling tanks and ore chutes. Operated in the early 1900s and again in the 1960s, it is an interesting place to camp and explore. Texture of weathered wood, wind eroded tailings, and tired, leaning structures are for artists and photographers. Small unsorted ore piles hold specimen material for rock collectors and somewhere in a nearby gully there should be a treasure of old bottles, but it will take some looking since the discards from the recent operation will have covered the older artifacts. This is hardly a place to expect rewards in a quick look around, and since the mine is on the windward side of Fremont Peak, it can be so uncomfortably cold any treasure hunting is probably out of the question.

From the Monarch-Rand Mine the dirt road market EF 411 heads west and is frequently intersected by good graded roads. It is approximately 7 miles straight out to Highway 395.

"On the Atcheson, Topeka . . ."

Within 6 miles from the mine ruins EF 411 crosses over the old railroad line going from Kramer Junction to Johannesburg. This was the Randsburg branch of the Atchison Topeka and Santa Fe Railroad. To the immediate left are the ruins of Fremont, one of the stations along the route.

Going another one mile from the Fremont ruins, EF 411 meets Highway 395. Approximately nine miles to the right is Atolia, the starting point. Remember, there are no gas stations in that area. To the left on Highway 395, in 13.6 miles, is Four Corners (Kramer Junction) with supplies, accommodations, and traffic. The quiet, relaxed mood country will be but a memory.

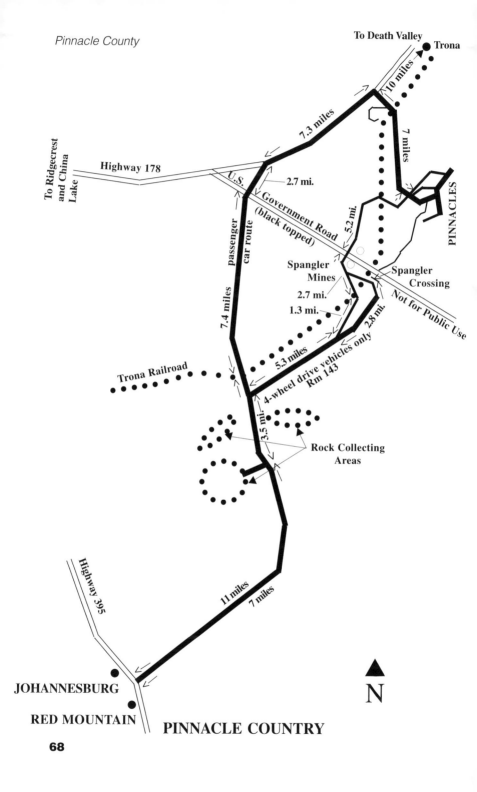

To Death Valley

Trona

10 miles

7.3 miles

7 miles

To Ridgecrest
and China
Lake

Highway 178

2.7 mi.

U.S.

Government Road
(black topped)

PINNACLES

5.2 mi.

passenger
car route

Spangler
Mines

Spangler
Crossing

2.7 mi.

1.3 mi.

Not for Public Use

7.4 miles

2.8 mi.

5.3 miles

4-wheel drive vehicles only
Rm 143

Trona Railroad

3.5 mi.

Rock Collecting
Areas

Highway 395

11 miles

7 miles

N

JOHANNESBURG

RED MOUNTAIN

PINNACLE COUNTRY

Pinnacle Country

Take off from reality and experience a hidden world of weird shapes and moving shadows. A one-way in and out passenger car trip or loop through the desert for more rugged vehicles is to be enjoyed during dry, cool weather.

M any years ago, before our astronauts had conquered space, 20th Century Fox used the Pinnacle country for a science fiction movie complete with scenes of the first family "landing on the moon." Movie patrons thought the whole thing was out of this world. In reality, anyone with a taste for adventure can enjoy this moon-like land without the discomfort of a space suit.

Fascinating figures, domes and steeples of white, tans, browns, faded red and gray cover an area over ten miles long and four miles wide. Depending on the time of day and lighting, the unique formations present an ever-changing panorama enhanced by shadow patterns. Visitors see many likenesses in the assortment of shapes and have named the larger ones: The Monk, Owl, Eagle and Dog, but the resemblances show only at certain times of the day, otherwise they appear as objects unknown to earth people.

An interesting area to explore many times, the Pinnacles lie between Red Mountain and Trona, dividing the stark white of Searles Lake from the tan-to-rose tones of the Mojave Desert. There is a well-defined road from the highway that is used by passenger cars, but the longer, back country route has a great deal more to offer in scenery, and historic ruins.

Leave Highway 395 one mile north of Red Mountain, at the sign indicating the turn off to Trona and Death Valley. A good, hard-surfaced road stretches out toward the valley and the blue haze of distant mountains. Near the summit, at seven miles from the junction, a dirt road drops off to the left. This side trail is hard packed, fine for car, camper, or small trailer and leads into a miniature canyon of volcanic pinks, tans and rich brick red. The area is an old gem rock picking field that has been searched for years yet still produces good, colorful cutting material. For the collector or non-collector the canyon is a delightful camping spot, fairly secluded yet within a few feet of the road.

Choice for Collectors

The terrain is sloping and the low rolling hills are for easy walking with an ever-changing material underfoot. For the rock collector there are small pieces, two to three cab size, variegated red agate with dendrite, good white-banded yellow jasper with brown, red or green plume. Jasp-agate from transparent to red, tan, deep wine with traces of green and yellow continuously erode out near an outcrop of Basalt containing very small agate geodes to the west of the road. Interesting green and red jasper is exposed in the low gray hills to the left near the entrance to the area and looks promising for one with an inclination to dig below the weathered top.

The amount of material to be found depends on the rate of erosion and this is not the place to collect large chunks or any great amount, but who needs a ton anyway? It takes too many lifetimes to work up!

Two and nine-tenths miles farther along the main highway or 9.9 miles from Highway 395, a ridge of decomposed jasper and agate can be seen on either side of the road. To the casual observer this is an uninteresting appearing jumble of broken rock, but for the collector with a fluorescent light there is the beauty of bright green, orange, and red that is hidden from the naked eye.

Off-Road Vehicle Route

Six-tenths of a mile further from this point or 10.5 miles from the junction of Highway 395 and the Trona Road, a dirt road turns right, before the main route you are on crosses the railroad tracks. A sign at this point says "TEAGLE Wash, Off-Road Vehicle Staging Area." The dirt road is marked with a BLM road marker RM 143. This is where modern cars with their soft springs will continue on the main highway while off-road vehicles can take to the dirt road. The dirt road is traveled by passenger cars but should not be attempted unless the driver is familiar with desert driving and the vehicle is of high clearance and capable of maneuvering a few sharp dips. For the most part this dirt road (RM 143) is clearly marked. RM 143 angles northeast for 6.7 miles along the south side of the railroad tracks and then crosses those tracks. One and two tenths miles on RM 143 from the Trona Road, a dirt road (RM 7) intersects RM 143. Do not take RM 7 but keep going straight on RM 143. Within an additional 2.9 miles or 4.1 miles from the Trona road, another dirt road (RM 7A) intersects RM 143. Do not take RM 7A either, but keep going straight on RM 143. Continuing on RM 143 for another 1.2 miles you come to a "Y" with a RM 143 BLM marker on the left. The right branch of the "Y" will be discussed later. Stay to the left on RM 143 for another 1.3 miles or 6.7 miles from the Trona Road and you are at the railroad crossing.

The rails that the road parallels is the Trona Railroad, one of the few short lines left in operation in the United States. It was built when mule team freighting could no longer haul borax in competition with companies near railroads. The Southern Pacific line was thirty-two miles away (see Summit trip - Chapter 4) and neither they nor any other company wanted to risk investing in a road to Trona where borax was being mined. The Trona company was desperate because their whole future hinged on transporting their product to the main line at a reasonable cost.

In spite of harassment by claim jumpers, legal battles over claim boundaries, labor problems created by the many races working at the lake and the need for plant development, the struggling young company decided to build their own line. Unlike most railroad construction of that time, there was no ribbon cutting, band playing, toast drinking, or colorful ground breaking ceremony. Different, too, was the fact that on September 27, 1913, the wife of the company president, Mrs. Joseph Hutchinson did the ground breaking. Dressed in high fashion, with large decorative hat, long sleeved blouse and a skirt that swept the ground she trudged behind a plow in the shimmering desert heat. The team of mules raised a cloud of dust that covered her beautiful attire and sand seeped into her high button shoes. Though the ceremony was unorthodox, the railroad thrived. It outlived many of the big lines and today hauls chemical wealth over its well kept 32 miles of track.

Engines of Another Era

Driving within sight of the rails most of the time, the visitor can mentally picture the early day train with its immense steam engines, open-windowed coaches, men standing in the open door of the mail car and others walking across the top of freight cars. The picturesque steam locomotive with its mixed load was replaced by diesel power in 1948, but if you are fortunate enough to be in the area when the short line train passes by, it will seem that old Number 2 is still in use. A white cloud flows back of the locomotive and along the ridge of cars like billowing smoke from a steam locomotive. The impression is the result of powdered chemicals whirling into the air from some of the open gondolas.

Thousands of tons of soda ash, chlorides of soda, lithium, pyro borate, borax and many by-products are hauled on this route daily. The old time table and schedule listed stops for ore shipments and passengers at Trona, Borosolvay (now West End), Rock Crusher, Hanksite, Pinnacle, Spangler and Searles. The only stops today between West End and Searles are in the spring when grazing sheep move out of the wind into sheltered coves and onto the tracks, or at night when a herd of wild burro decides to feed on the other side of the tracks, stringing out in plodding determination that brings the heavy loaded cars to a stop.

One and two-tenths miles past the intersection of RM 7A or 5.3 miles from the Trona Road you will come to a "Y" as mentioned above. The left branch marked RM 143 crosses the railroad tracks 1.3 miles further. This is 6.7 miles from the Trona Road. The right branch is the old road that crosses the railroad tracks at the old Spangler train stop 2.8 miles further. If you take the old road (right branch), go 2.7 miles further and on the right will be a mound of dirt (mining remains) with a railroad tie standing vertical. A faint road to the left goes 0.1 miles to the railroad crossing.

At this point you can clearly see the several Tamarisk trees at the site of the old railroad water tower at Spangler. The railroad track crossing is 8.1 miles from the Trona Road.

Just Enough Gold

In this area you will find the Spangler ruins where two brothers, Rea and Tony, spent the major portions of their lives digging by hand thousands of feet in underground tunnels. The gold they brought out was never enough to make them wealthy, but paid for food and supplies, and was sufficient to tease them into making "just one more try." By following the newer route (RM 143) you will miss the ruins and cross the tracks a mile sooner, putting you on the north side.

For those who are at Spangler, cross the railroad tracks going north and proceed up the road 0.8 miles to the intersection with RM 143. The road is faint and filled with bike tracks. It is quite sandy. This road should not be attempted by two-wheel drive vehicles. Cross the good dirt road (RM 143) and you are 1.3 miles beyond the railroad track crossing. For those who remained on RM 143, and did not take the trip to Spangler, go 1.3 miles past the crossing where the Tamarisk trees come into view down on the railroad tracts to the right.

Two and seven-tenths miles further on route RM 143 (from its crossing of the railroad tracks or 1.4 miles further if you took the Spangler side trip and you are now back on RM 143) visitors cross the paved U.S. Government Road. Signs clearly state that you are not to use the U.S. Government Road. Crossing the government road, a sign announces seven miles to the Pinnacles following RM 143. Actually it is 5.2 miles to the edge of the Pinnacles. When you cross the railroad tracks, within 0.2 miles on the right is the first road leading to the Pinnacles. If you continue on RM 143, it stays close to the railroad tracks. Within another 1.7 miles and to the right is the main road into the Pinnacles area. From this point north, lumps of rough porous looking rock begin to appear. In the distance can be seen larger formations marching along the rim of a smooth basin. Freighters skirted those formations over 100 years ago. Seeing a resemblance to church steeples, they called the place Cathedral City. Later the official name, Pinnacles, appeared on maps.

Fall Tufa

These unique formations were built up under a lake when the area was tropical and fresh water flowed into the sink now known as Searles Dry Lake. The formations are spread over an area 3 miles wide and 4.5 miles long. There are more than 500 tufa (calcium carbonate) pinnacles. Some are as high as 140 feet above the lake bed. The ancient beach line is visible about 700 hundred feet above the present desert and dry lake surface which shows one how deep the lake was at one time. The Pinnacles were formed under water 10,000 to 100,000 years ago by the interaction of blue-green algae, minute organisms growing one upon another, and a combination of chemical and geothermal conditions. The lake had limited outflow and there was considerable mineral rich runoff from local geothermal sites. Thus the lake became a concentrated area of carbonate brine. Underground hot springs in the lake introduced calcium rich ground water. When this was combined with the carbonates, calcium carbonate deposits were formed. With the blue-green algae bonding with the calcium carbonate, they formed the shapes that stand dry and rough surfaced along the desert floor. At that time, Searles Lake was part of a chain of Pleistocene lakes. At the northern end was the Owens Valley and at the southern end was Death Valley. These lakes were all interconnected. In 1968, the Department of Interior designated the Trona Pinnacles as a National Natural Landmark. Today the Trona Pinnacles are managed by the Bureau of Land Management.

Passenger Car Route

For the passenger car traveler, the trip to the same area is 28.4 miles from the highway junction out of Red Mountain to the turnoff to the Pinnacles. Eleven miles from Highway 395 on the Trona Road you cross the railroad tracks. Another 7.4 miles or 18.4 miles from Highway 395 you cross the U.S. Government Road which connects two U.S. Government installations. Private vehicles are not permitted on this road. Another 2.7 miles or 21.1 miles from Highway 395 is the intersection of Highway 178 out of Ridgecrest. Turn right and after another 7.3 miles you are at the turnoff to the Pinnacles.

A right turn onto a dirt road at the highway sign "End 178" has another sign saying the Pinnacles are ahead seven miles. The dirt road is marked as BLM road RM 143. The road is well traveled as Trona residents have been frequent visitors to the Pinnacles. After a rain, the road may be impassable to all vehicles. If in question about the road conditions into the Pinnacles, check with the Ridgecrest Resource Area Office of The Bureau of Land Management at (760) 375-7125. Within a little over a mile the road crosses the Trona railroad tracks and a sharp right hand turn (there is usually a "Pinnacle" sign at this point) takes the visitor to the start of the picturesque formations in less than four miles. The route crosses a lake bed that is slippery when wet and makes it advisable to visit during dry weather. Because it follows the rolling contour of the land, speed exceeding 20 miles per hour is not practical in many places. There is primitive camping allowed at the Pinnacles and campers are encouraged to use existing camp sites and fire rings. You need to bring your own firewood and camping is limited to 14 days.

Surface of the Moon

A maze of roads weave in and out of the formations giving ever-changing viewpoints. Morning and evening coloring is the most intense and the long blue shadows of the late or early hours adds much to the beauty of the area. This is moon country without a space suit or the trauma of a splash down, with the highway only seven miles away. You have a choice of left to Red Mountain and Ridgecrest or right 10 miles to the center of Trona. After you have explored the area, passenger car travelers will back track to the paved highway. If you take RM 143 from the Trona Highway there is the continuation of RM 143 on the north east side of the Pinnacles, follow this road out to the paved highway.

Trona with its modern facilities is an ideal place to stop before or after visiting the Pinnacles, or preparing for an extended trip to Death Valley. Each year on Columbus Day weekend, Trona holds its Gem-O-Rama, which is sponsored by the Searles Lake Gem & Mineral Society. This stop is a definite must for people traveling at that time of year.

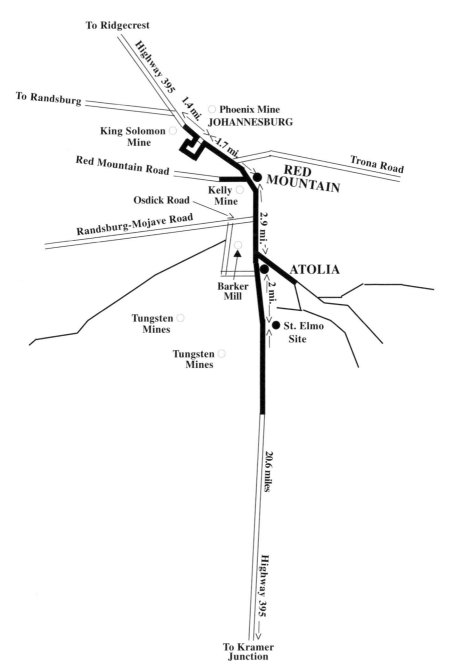

ATOLIA, RED MOUNTAIN, AND JOHANNESBURG

7

Atolia, Red Mountain, and Johannesburg

In and around desert towns that are but a faint shadow of their flourishing beginnings. This trip is accessible with any type of vehicle.

R emember the last time you slowed down to a posted speed limit and loafed through the few blocks of a small town, all the while wondering why it existed?

There are a number of such miniature communities along Highway 395 as it climbs northward to skirt the east side of the Sierras. Outwardly most of them offer little to entice the traveler into taking time out from his or her rush to some distant destination. Yet each has its story, points of interest and reason for being. Usually the settlements are many miles apart or at least a day's travel by team and wagon; an exception is a cluster of four desert communities separated by only two to four miles.

From the intersection of the east-west artery of State Highway 58 and U.S. Highway 395 at Kramer Junction (Four Corners) the route north cuts through miles of seemingly uninhabited desert. Fremont Peak on the right, Red Mountain almost straight ahead and the Federal Prison facility on the left are all that break up the sameness of near-level desert acres. The modern, high speed road parallels the old roadbed of a Santa Fe Railroad branch that took one hour and 25 minutes for the run of 28.5 miles into the gold, silver and tungsten country. The first stop for water, freight and passengers was Fremont, almost opposite the mountain by the same name.

Tungsten Boom and Bust

Twenty and six-tenths miles from Kramer Junction was St. Elmo that is marked now by the rusted remains of tin cans, and bits of broken glass located two miles south of Atolia. A little less than 80 years ago that area became the largest tungsten producing field in the world, and St. Elmo faded out as Atolia became the center of activity. One of the four closely related settlements, Atolia has boomed and died more than once depending on the need for tungsten. Through it all, miners kept some of the buildings in repair, hung onto their leases and hoped for prices that compensated for their labor.

The handful of buildings that is Atolia lies on both sides of the highway. The first set of buildings on the right is a large mining operation 22.6 miles north of Kramer Junction or 7.1 miles south of the Randsburg cutoff and Highway 395. A metal gate on the right closes off one mining operations section and a cable on the left shuts an old road leaving only an entrance to the company offices.

Three-tenths of a mile further north from the mine entrance metal gate on the right side of the road, just before the blue call box #395-692, is part of a foundation that marks the site of the one-time Donker's Sunshine Dairy. It was known for its non-fat milk long before that type of milk was an accepted product. Though mothers worried about the value to their children, there was little they could do except complain as fresh milk was a scarce item on the desert. Interesting jugs with sturdy bales and an occasional glass milk bottle emblazoned with name were once recovered intact, protected by the overhanging branches of native bushes.

On the right just a short distance north (0.4 miles) from the mining operation's metal gate (or 0.1 miles from the Sunshine Dairy foundation) is a dirt road that dips off the highway and heads for more mining country, an old cattle spread, abandoned homestead sites, Fremont Peak, and military reservations; all of which are another area to explore (see Chapter 5).

For a short mile trip into the immediate area, follow this good graded dirt road for 0.4 miles and turn right on another dirt road for

0.4 miles and you will come upon a picturesque head frame which is immediately visible when you turn off of Highway 395. There is adequate space for parking and turning around. Just before reaching the head frame, you pass the edge of a pit and buildings further to the right which is the Old Spanish Mine. Here, in the rows of cone-shaped mounds and man-made canyons, wealth in tungsten was produced.

Hope Still Lingers

The Old Spanish Mine, one of the first big strikes in the field, was discovered and developed by a group of Spanish-speaking miners. They kept to themselves, made a fortune, and departed. Various miners worked the existing tunnels and added more; some did well, others found little for their trouble and some died of injuries from falling rocks. In the early 1970s a search for a new ore bed was in full swing and signs of a possible bonanza were present, but further blasting failed to locate that which was hoped for. The miners moved on in the continuous quest for a pay streak. It will again be leased to someone who has a theory about where the values lie and that person may be the one to hit the jackpot and set off another mining boom. Maybe they will quit a winner, but more than likely history will repeat itself with the earnings poured back into the ground in the hope that a still richer deposit will be found.

Going back to the intersection of the dirt road and Highway 395, turn right and go north another 1.1 miles where the old Santa Fe Railroad roadbed is plainly visible on the right as is the scattered dump of the early 1900s that in recent years became a favored hunting ground for relic hunters.

On the hill to the left is the Barker Mill, built many years ago by one of the Barker brothers of the well known Los Angeles furniture merchants. Like the Atolia mining, the mill had been in operation off and on, depending on the market for tungsten. Almost in line with the mill is the old dirt road (now gated) that climbed to the mill. If you drive north another 0.9 miles, turn left onto Osdick Road and drive up the paved road a short distance for a good view of the Barker Mill on the left. To the right are the spectacular structures associated with the Kelly Silver Mine and mill on the outskirts of Red Mountain.

Within a mile from Highway 395 Osdick Road branches left

to Butte Avenue, which is just past a cluster of buildings, then curves back towards Atolia and ends next to the cable-closed entrance to Highway 395. At the junction with Butte Avenue, Osdick Road has turned into the Randsburg-Mojave Road that goes to California City, a trip discussed in Chapter 3. From this one mile paved road which becomes dirt for the remainder of the way, there are numerous good, car-passable, dirt roads that wander through miles of diggings, dumps and occasional campsites where a diligent search can turn up an aged sun-purpled bottle, a tobacco tin, discarded toy or heavy miner's pick (minus the wooden handle). Stick to the most traveled road and within 2.5 miles you will be back on Highway 395 having gone the back way back to Atolia.

Silver Ghosts

Instead of going behind the mountains back to Atolia, visitors can turn around on Osdick Road and return to Highway 395. Turn left onto Highway 395 and continue north for 0.5 miles to Red Mountain Road. Turn left and go up the road a short distance to the remains of the old Kelly Mine. The Kelly was a large, rich silver operation that supported its own mill. Well-built company houses are still occupied and kept in good repair by local residents. The buildings of the milling operation stand in ruins, gaunt silhouettes against the clear desert sky.

Remains of the Kelly Silver Mine buildings and tailings as seen from Highway 395 and Red Mountain Road.

The skeleton of the large building, the cream colored sump, and the molded residue left by dismantled tanks, offer the photographer, amateur or professional, an immense variety to record on film. The Kelly developed from a fabulously rich silver deposit that gold seekers had been stumbling over for years while trying to eke out a living. Some of the men were nearly starving on the little gold they could produce while at the same time they were throwing away and cussing the dark, troublesome metal that interfered with their work. It was in 1919 that two curious prospectors had samples assayed that were so high in silver content that it left California gasping and set off another boom in an area already famous for its gold and tungsten. Typical of mining discoveries, the miners poured in hoping to find a small bit of unclaimed land to work for themselves or get in on the jobs opening with the growing company. Most settled for any and all available jobs and were happy to be at work in the business they knew best. Mining was slow all over the west and miners had found it difficult to stay employed.

The Kelly welcomed the miners, and although there were no living accommodations, that condition changed with unbelievable speed. Tents were pitched in scattered disarray, empty buildings from Johannesburg, Randsburg and as far away as Garlock, were cut into movable pieces and rushed to the scene. Even before they were off the moving-timbers buildings went into use and a line of businessplaces formed along an unplanned street.

The boom brought in all types of men. Highgrading of the rich silver was an accepted fact, fights were the order of the day and shootings frequently went unnoticed. Water was scarce, but a drink of liquor could be obtained everyplace except the post office, where there were problems enough without serving drinks.

Sin City

As the population burgeoned, a feud developed between two factions. Pete Osdick, a long time resident miner who had been scratching for gold almost on the door step of the Kelly, attempted to build an orderly, law-abiding settlement named Osdick. The other faction tended toward the wild, roaring mine camp pattern and went by various names including Inn City and Sin City.

The post office, caught in the middle of the controversy and trying to settle on one name for mail delivery, finally disregarded local opinion and, using the imposing mountain overlooking all the activity, called it Red Mountain. If the outside world or newcomers gave it any thought the name probably seemed appropriate, but some of the local residents resented the postal highhandedness to their dying day.

By whatever name one wanted to call it, the town was a wild, wide open place resembling the old mine camps of the late 1800s. Liquor flowed freely until word came that the "revonoers" were coming to make a raid. The closure lasted only until the law was seen going down the dusty road. Madams ran houses that were small replicas of the Barbary Coast days and clients came from as far away as Los Angeles. The dance hall girls were pretty and as one bartender recalled, "They were mostly brunettes, a few red heads and no blonds."

Time and fires have wiped out much of Red Mountain's wild past; the mine buildings, the dumps of green, gold, blue and pink and a few miners' shacks that have been modernized are of that past. Saloons, hotels and cribs that were the town's backbone of activity are mostly gone. Some that remain have been changed beyond recognition such as the Owl Saloon and Hotel and the Silver Dollar, a replacement that saw only the dwindling action at the end of the boom era. At the time of this printing, The Owl Saloon and Hotel is now the Old Owl Cottages (a Bed and Breakfast) and Cottontail Antiques. Located 0.3 miles north of Osdick Road or 0.2 miles south of Red Mountain Road, the establishment is located on the west side of Highway 395. Slim's Cottage (sleeps 1-7 guests) and Bessie's Honeymoon Cottage (sleeps 2 guests). For information or reservations call (888) 653-6953 (toll free) or Fax (760) 374-2354. A little further north on the left side of Highway 395 in Red Mountain, next to Red Mountain Road, is the Silver Dollar Saloon which recently has been turned into an antique store.

Golfing Around the Gold Mills

One and seven tenths miles north of Red Mountain, Highway 395 enters Johannesburg, the only settlement of the four closely related mining communities whose growth was planned rather than a hit or miss happenstance. In the early years its greatest boast was the golf club where members played a course that ran around the outskirts of the town. It must have been an interesting sight as men in caps and knickers, women in long skirts, high-necked blouses and wide-brimmed hats battled the wind and sand to the tune of the heavy thumping beat of gold mills hammering rock into dust.

A left turn at the old St. Charles Hotel (on the right side of the intersection of The Rand Road and Highway 395) takes visitors past Teagle's store (across the street and on the right side of the intersection of the Rand Road and Randsburg Road) from which supplies were freighted to the mine camps in the Panamints, Skidoo and Death Valley. Appearing to be part of the same building but with a different false front, is what had been Harrison's Saloon where shooting scrapes were always in self defense and Harrison was deemed justified in doing whatever he wished.

At the intersection of the Rand Road and Panamint Street (on the right side) is a house that originally was the top half of the railroad station. Surprisingly, it has lost none of its depot look. Higher up the hill, Mt. Wells Avenue (0.5 miles from Highway 395), turning to the right and 2 blocks down the street, swings around the cemetery that for 100 years has served the desert for miles around. Sand blasted wooden head boards and ornate iron fences stand in contrast to the more recent unique rock work erected in memory of Shady Myrick, the discoverer of Myrickite, a gem rock that was highly prized by rock collectors. Another pretentious edifice nearby is for Burro Schmidt, the man who spent a good portion of his lifetime digging a tunnel through a mountain in the El Paso range.

Beyond the cemetery is the remains of the once great King Solomon Mine that was discovered in 1896. Exact gold output is unknown, but records show that between 1919 and 1942 it produced approximately $500,000 with gold running $25 per ton of ore from its vast underground network that reaches to the Big Butte Mine in Randsburg. Silence engulfs the place today and one's foot step will echo through the empty buildings where noise, crushed rock, dust, shouting men and the grind of machinery live only in memory. Backtracking to Highway 395 and turning left going north, the Randsburg cutoff from Highway 395 is 1.4 miles.

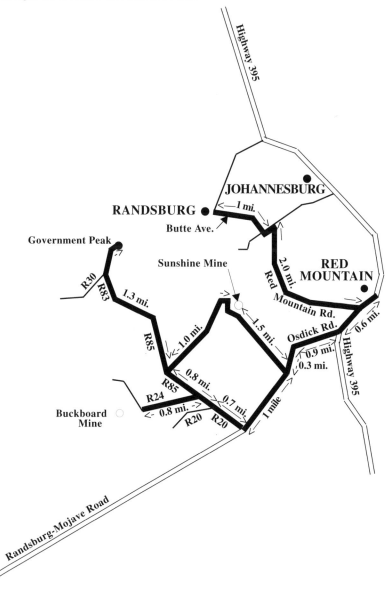

N

STRINGER DISTRICT AND GOVERNMENT PEAK

Stringer District and Government Peak

This area, like a majority of the Mojave Desert, is best explored during cool weather. Passenger cars can safely travel most of the roads. Directions are indicated for trails that are only for more sturdy vehicles.

An almost unbelievably short time ago (a little more than 125 years) few men had put foot on the Rand Mountains. There were no wagon wheel ruts or mine scars, not even a name. Wild plants and animal life thrived undisturbed in the valley, along the ridges and down the multi-forked washes.

The whole scene changed in 1895 with the discovery of gold on the north side of the unexplored range. What was to become the famous Yellow Aster Mine triggered an influx of prospectors who spread through the canyon and swarmed over the hills sampling rock, running gravel through dry washers or with just a shovel and gold pan, decided where they thought a fortune may lay hidden.

A high, cone-shaped pile of rock marked each corner of the chunk of desert each man or group of men selected. Mine claims like the squares, triangles and oblong pieces of a patchwork quilt covered miles of mountains, canyons and washes. Some found enough gold to warrant extensive development, but the majority of the men flowing into the area had to settle for jobs in established mines or move on to continue their restless search for the illusive metal.

A trip from the main street of Randsburg going east to the opposite side of the mountain is to travel the ghost country of gold dominated years. The Stringer District is a visual example of man's determination to wrest wealth from the earth. The pitted and bruised land is mute evidence of gold's relentless power.

Echoes of Fiddler's Gulch

As Butte Avenue climbs to the outskirts of town it passes between a couple of one-time sizeable mine operations. Big Butte stretches along the mountain side on the left and Consolidated pushes up a draw on the right. Travel east through the now silent Fiddler's Gulch. The few standing head frames, eroded tailings and tunnel openings are small reminders of the boom days when men, teams, dynamite blasts and the continuous thump of stamp mills made it a busy, noisy place.

One mile from Randsburg, the paved road swings to the left. The road to the right goes to the entrance of The Rand Mining Company. Two tenths of a mile further, the road splits with Randsburg Loop to the left and Red Mountain Road to the right. Take Red Mountain Road and around the corner is a dirt road heading to the right up a slight hill. At the top is a large display and viewing area of the operations of the Rand Mining Company. This is a most impressive sight. After visiting the viewing center, return to Red Mountain Road and continue down the hill for another 1.3 miles to Highway 395 and the southern edge of the town of Red Mountain. Just before reaching Highway 395 on the right are the picturesque remains of the Kelly Silver Mine discussed in Chapter 7.

To explore the Stringer Mining District, turn right on Highway 395 and go south for 0.6 miles to Osdick Road. Turn right and go up the hill on the dirt road. The road becomes paved within a short distance and the paved portion turns left on Butte Avenue 0.9 miles from Highway 395. Don't take the left branch, but continue on the dirt road which is now the Randsburg-Mojave Road. Continuing for another 0.3 miles or 1.2 miles from Highway 395, turn right onto a good graded road going up a gentle incline in a north westerly direction. Straight ahead the ruins of the Sunshine Mine are visible as are the towers on top of Government Peak.

The Sunshine Mine ruins are 1.5 miles from this turnoff.

Within 0.2 miles a "Y" is encountered with the good graded road staying on the left and a lesser quality road going to the right. Stay to the left on the good graded road, cross a power line road then proceed straight up the gentle rise. Within another 0.5 miles ignore two additional roads that intersect the graded road to the Sunshine Mine. Go another 0.6 miles, passing the caretaker's house on the right, to reach the top of the hill. To the left and right are the remains of the Sunshine Mine, just 1.5 miles from the turnoff from the Randsburg-Mojave Road. An old tank, tailing piles and vandalized shaft are all that is left of an operation that followed a six to 12 inch wide, 600 foot deep vein of gold-bearing quartz.

Golden Grains

Wheat-sized grains of gold, some of the largest mined in the Rand Mountains, were brought out of the Sunshine from 1896 to 1915. A three-stamp mill and cyanide plant processed the ore that ran one and a half ounces of gold per ton of ore and produced $1,000,000 in the nineteen-year period.

The next stop is Government Peak from where a spectacular view of the surrounding area and the Rand Mining Company's

All that remains of the once active Sunshine Mine.

operation is visible. There are two ways to get there. The first is the most interesting road in terms of viewing old mining sites. From the top of the hill at the Sunshine Mine go 0.1 miles further on the dirt road and turn left where the road deadends at the Rand Mining Company fence line. Go left for 0.1 miles and just before the gate of the Rand Mining Company is reached turn left again. The road is narrower and goes initially up a small hill. Within a half mile there is considerable evidence of mining on all sides.

This is a good place to park and explore on foot. In accordance with the law all abandoned mine excavations have been covered, closed and fenced, but there are thoughtless individuals who remove covers, make campfires out of the fencing and tear down tunnel closures. The danger is minimal but it takes only one fall to spoil a trip. Counsel children against running or straying away from adults. Common sense dictates the futility of standing on the edge of a hole to peer down into black nothingness.

Broken Veins

The area so extensively mined, was composed of a network of narrow veins or stringers carrying gold and tungsten throughout an otherwise non-metallic rock mass. The veins, though usually rich in ore, were not only narrow but were frequently offset or broken by fault lines. Considerable extra digging had to be done in search of stringers that suddenly stopped. It took all of a miner's past experience, some guess work and a good portion of luck, hope and hard work in sleuthing underground for that lost thread of ore.

Heavily worked from 1896 to 1918, the area is not only strewn with old wood and rusted metal, but the broken pieces of sun purpled glass suggest that old bottles and other artifacts may be buried in the gullies or within throwing distance of old cabin sites. At present there is little evidence of relic digging, yet occupancy dates back to the liquor, cod liver oil and patent medicine period that quickens the pulse of the bottle collector.

As interesting as the ruins are some of the mine names that run the full gamut from the unimaginative G.B. Mine, to the more colorful Orphan Girl, Winnie, Red Bird, Sophie Moren, Pearl Wedge, Ben Hur and Tam-O-Shanter. The Gold Crown, Gold Coin, Gold King, Victory Wedge, and Golden Eagle seemed to be more wishful than actual.

Radio on the Rocks

From this mine-pitted locality the road continues south-westerly through scattered workings and rock cabin ruins. It is a firm surfaced road but a couple of short dips within the next 0.5 miles are sharp enough to cause low slung passenger car rear bumpers to scrape. For those continuing beyond this point there is directional assurance in the almost continuous view on the right of the various transmitters on top of Government Peak. Lesser used roads branch to the right into more abandoned diggings and an area that carries highgrade manganese with rhodonite, most of which is on privately owned claims.

There are two routes to reach Government Peak. One mile from the Rand Mining Company gate, a good graded road is intersected. Turn right onto this road going up a gentle grade. Mine tailings are visible straight ahead. The road is marked with a BLM road marker - R85. Continuing on this road, it is 1.3 miles to the base of Government Peak.

One mile up the road, R83 joins at this point from the left. Keep going straight ahead on R83. Within another 0.2 miles, R83 intersects R30. Turn right onto R30 for 0.1 miles, and the base of Government Peak is reached which is on the left side of the road. Stop at this point. It is less than 0.5 miles to the crest of Government Peak.

The second route to Government Peak from the Sunshine Mine is to back track 1.5 miles from the Sunshine Mine down the good graded dirt road to the Randsburg-Mojave Road. When reached, turn right heading west for one mile. Turn right onto the BLM marked road - R20. There is a large BLM sign saying "Rand Mountain - Fremont Valley." From here it is 2.8 miles up the road to Government Peak. Within 0.7 miles from the Randsburg-Mojave Road, a "Y" is reached. R20 goes straight while the good graded road goes right up the hill and is now called R85. Stay to the right on R85 until it joins R83.

Keep going straight ahead on R83. Within another 0.2 miles, R83 intersects R30. Turn right onto R30 for 0.1 miles and the base of Government Peak is reached. Stop at this point. It is less than 0.5 miles to the crest of Government Peak.

This 4,755-foot high point in the Rand Range bristles with

towers that are a part of government and telephone utility communication systems. Though the road continues to the peak and the fenced structures, there is little space for parking or turning around, so it is advisable to walk the remainder of the distance if one desires a view from the top which has little advantage over the panorama seen from the lower level. There is a deep rut as the road starts up the hill. In no case should passenger cars, mini vans or other low profile vehicles attempt the trip to the top. In either case the scene is like an aerial photo that encompasses great distances and offers a new perspective of the country to be explored.

To the far northwest is the snow-topped southern portion of the Sierras. Closer in, note the El Paso Mountains that run northeast to southwest and skirt the flat expanse of Fremont Valley. Miles of desert tan are interrupted by the white of Koehn Dry Lake, small green squares of alfalfa, dark clumps of tamarisk trees and the thin lines that mark old freight routes or the more recent trails cut by off-road vehicles.

Reached by Rocky Roads

On either side of Government Peak can be seen abandoned mine camps that cling to the mountainside and can be reached only by narrow foot or wagon trails. The buildings are collapsing, tunnels caving and erosion is eating away the long unused roads. Any one of them would be an interesting place to visit if one is inclined to enjoy long distance hiking over rough, steep terrain punctuated by slide areas. Directly to the north and east is a spectacular view of the large open-pit mining operation of the Rand Mining Company.

To the east a lone peak rising out of the gold-toned expanse of Cuddeback Dry Lake and Golden Valley is the early explorer's landmark, Fremont Peak. Blue haze and indistinct mountains 70 miles away are the San Bernardino Mountains that form a border along the edge of this desert picture.

The next stop on this trip is a visit to the picturesque Buckboard Mine. To get there from the base of Government Peak, backtrack down the hill on the good graded road that was used to get to the top. The trip down is 1.7 miles to the intersection of R24. This means heading back up the hill 0.1 miles on R30 to the intersection with R83. Turn left down the hill on R83 and when it intersects with R85 keep going down the hill on R85 past R22 and then stop when R24 is reached. Turn right and the Buckboard Mine is 0.8 miles. Within 0.6 miles a cross road is reached with R83 going right and R22 going left. This occurs in a wash. Go across and up the hill following R24 up the canyon for another 0.2 miles to the Buckboard Mine. If the vehicle can't go up the hill, then follow R83 to the right up the road for 0.2 miles. Stop and walk up the wash on the left hand side of the road. The Buckboard is up the wash about 100 feet.

Slanting Shafts

Looking back, a complete headframe silhouettes against the distant valley on one side and sage-covered banks on the other. Three openings to incline shafts smile defiance at explorer, photographer and relic collector. The shafts slant to a 450-foot depth plus 2000 feet of drifts all of which add up to a sizeable amount of underground blasting and digging. The miners followed a gold-bearing fault along a footwall of a rhyolite dike that produced $500,000 in gold and an unknown amount of tungsten. In the area, there are a number of other mine shafts.

From the old Buckboard the road climbs and thins out to a single track between steep canyon walls. Outcrops of quartz, manganese and layers of mica shist resemble some of the material that the Buckboard shafts encountered underground and indicate the possibility of jewelry-quality rhodonite in the near vicinity.

When finished exploring this area, return to the main dirt road by following R24 back to R85 and turn right. Follow R85 down the hill past the intersection with R20 and take R20 back to the Randsburg-Mojave Road which is a total of 1.1 miles from R24. On the way down note the many side roads that are available for exploring. This is the edge of the Atolia tungsten field which overlapped into the Stringer gold and tungsten deposit. Though the car miles are surprisingly few, the Stringer area is large in its offerings for leisurely exploring. For those wanting to return to Highway 395 without exploring the side roads, turn left on the intersection of the Randsburg-Mojave Road, and Highway 395 is within 2.2 miles.

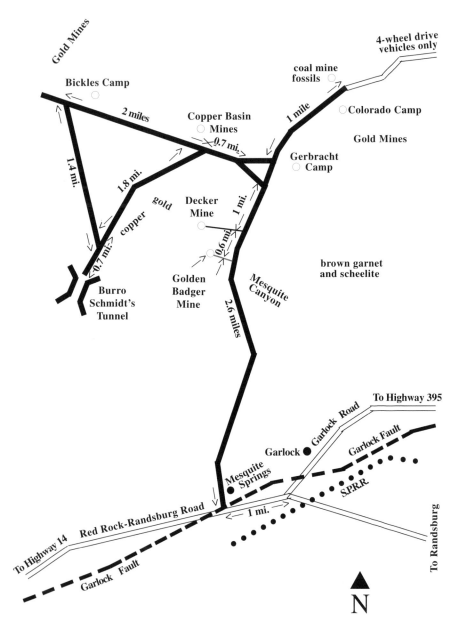

Bonanza Gulch

Gold Mines

Bickles Camp

2 miles

1.4 mi.

1.8 mi.

copper

gold

Copper Basin
Mines

0.7 mi.

Decker
Mine

0.7 mi.

Burro
Schmidt's
Tunnel

Golden
Badger
Mine

1 mi.

0.6 mi.

2.6 miles

Mesquite
Canyon

coal mine
fossils

4-wheel drive
vehicles only

Colorado Camp

Gold Mines

1 mile

Gerbracht
Camp

brown garnet
and scheelite

To Highway 395

Garlock Road

Garlock

Garlock Fault

S.P.R.R.

Mesquite
Springs

Red Rock-Randsburg Road

To Highway 14

Garlock Fault

1 mi.

To Randsburg

N

MESQUITE CANYON ROAD

Mesquite Canyon Road

Old mine camps, a mile-long tunnel, rock and fossil collecting, and camping spots along a good dirt road in Black Mountain country make good traveling in Fall, Winter, and Spring.

Some of the most picturesque desert characters of the Rand mining period traveled Mesquite Canyon enroute to their mine camps in the El Paso Range. They carved their own unique niche in history without striking a hoped-for bonanza that would have catapulted them into millionaires.

Early in the 1800s prospectors, following an old Indian foot path, worked their way up the narrow canyon searching the steep side slopes and small branching washes. Some found gold in or near the canyon while others went on to penetrate deeper into the unnamed mountains. By the 1850s the canyon was a pack route; sure-footed burros brought out gold concentrates and carried back the miner's supplies.

At the mouth of the canyon was a large cluster of mesquite trees that made it an easily identifiable spot and gave the canyon its name. A good sized stream of fresh spring water flowed toward the valley floor; grass and trees both thrived in the wet soil. It was an ideal rest area and rendezvous for miners and passing freight wagons. Gold was sent into the Los Angeles market and on the return trip the freighter would have the miner's order of food and equipment.

Hard to Gain, Easy to Lose

Every ounce of gold extracted from rock or ancient stream bed signified many hours of hard work which could be lost in a moment to ruthless outlaws. Renegades freely came and went through the canyon with no law except the miner's own ability to protect himself and his property. This state of affairs was not unique to Mesquite Canyon; it was the accepted hazard of the desert and mountains.

The outside world seldom heard of the atrocities, but occasionally via freighters the word reached the settlements. It was in 1864 that the owner of the Yarbrough Gold and Silver Company was found murdered at Mesquite Springs while he waited with a shipment of gold concentrates. A few days later men at two mines up above Mesquite Canyon were run off, and forty tons of rich gold ore, worth four hundred dollars a ton, was stolen.

Guns and highgrading were still prominent in Mesquite Canyon until a very few years ago. Many an innocent traveler looked into the yawning black depth of a gun barrel for no other reason than he dared be in the canyon. The canyon that started as a pack trail (and not too friendly to strangers) is now quiet. Residents are friendly and the road can easily be negotiated by modern passenger cars except when heavy rains or flash flooding turn the road into an escape route.

Since the canyon has become a popular access route to almost limitless mountain and valley exploration, four-wheel drive vehicles, pickups and bikes soon recondition any areas cut by rains, and all type vehicles can safely travel the entire length of the canyon. There are no sharp curves or sand traps and only a couple of short, low gear grades. It is by no means a speedway, but at a leisurely pace, avoiding gravel-piled shoulders and parking on solid ground, this canyon takes the explorer into the back country for a day or as long as his schedule will permit.

To reach Mesquite Canyon take the paved Red Rock-Randsburg road at the west end of Randsburg for 8.6 miles down into Fremont Valley. Crossing the railroad tracks, turn left at the stop sign and go for one mile. The entrance to the canyon is on the right with BLM road signs stating EP 100.

Within a mile from the paved highway, prospect holes are a frequent site along the mountain slope, and a short hike up any of the side washes will reveal others. Most are only a few feet deep where the prospector found "color" and dug a short way in hopes that it would develop into a sizeable gold deposit. He usually quit when ore indications pinched out or completely disappeared.

Two and six-tenths miles from the paved highway, a foot trail leads to the left up a narrow wash. About 400 feet up the wash is the old Golden Badger which produced unknown amounts of gold with only a record in 1940 of $4,000 for the year. For the rock collector there are showy seams of azurite and malachite in a nearby vein of copper-bearing quartz.

Only for the Willing

The next wash on the left, which is 2.8 miles from the high-way, has a narrow, eroded old wagon road, across which had been strung a cable. The very rough road goes up a steep incline to the Decker diggings. It is a most interesting place to visit, but only for those able and willing to climb by foot the almost perpendicular half mile, or drive up in a small four-wheel drive vehicle. Decker has long been gone, the old cabin is falling down, and the dry wash-ers, made of apple boxes and scrap lumber are gone as well as the old consumption remedy bottles that used to lie in piles back of the cabin.

Decker's cabin, like many other miner's shacks, was built near the mouth of his mine on the discard dump which was the only level place in the wash. Unlike other camps, this miner gouged a zigzag open-top tunnel in the opposite direction from the mine opening. The tunnel ends abruptly in a most unique sanitary facil-ity on the side of the mountains, with rock walls, rock floor, rock seat and blue sky for the roof.

Decker's claims like many others on the same side of the can-yon have not been worked for years, even the names have been forgotten except by old timers who still recall that the Side Hill Wedge should have produced better, or that the Old Look Out prob-ably gave up more gold than any outsider ever knew about. There was the Golden Eagle, Twin Brothers, Still Lower Half, McGowan's Gold, all silent ghosts of a long ago mining period.

A mile farther on the Mesquite road tops a ridge and the view is spectacular! Massive Black Mountain with multi-toned, eroded sides, lies straight ahead. To the left is a teasing glimpse of Last Chance Canyon and a distant panorama in blue, grays and lavenders as the Sierras stretch into the distance.

From Mines to Microwaves

A good road to the right is only a service road to a microwave station and deadends shortly. Keep straight ahead on EP 100 past the sign designating Gerbracht Camp for about one hundred yards and then take the road to the right (EP 262 and EP 15) which swings around the camp. For many years the name Gerbracht struck a note of fear in those who traveled the area. To local residents she was known as Della, respected for her knowledge and collection of minerals, disliked for her habit of grabbing mine claims, and feared for the gun she carried and used. When a shot came out of nowhere, and whined too close for comfort, there was usually little doubt as to who was attempting to scare one out of the canyon.

As the years went on, Della became more possessive of the canyons and the El Paso range; innocent travelers were shot at and some were wounded. The few remaining miners carried guns and told of having a feeling of being watched as they moved in and out of the canyon. Della is now gone, and today's visitors can travel unmolested.

The road (EP 262 and EP 15) from the Gerbracht Camp east should only be taken by high clearance vehicles. It passes between Black Mountain on the left and rolling, vegetation covered mountains on the right. Years that there have been winter or spring rains, this area, like Mesquite Canyon, is a flower garden from March to June. Acres of white, yellow, lavender and misty pink become great waves of color as light breezes keep each flower in motion. For the student of desert flora, the variety reaches from the stately Joshua to the mini-flowers at ground level with their smaller-than-pinhead size blooms.

In just over a mile the road tops a rise, and the ruins of Colorado Camp lie ahead. Vandals burned the interesting old rock and wood house, knocked down the bunk houses, destroyed or carried away mine and well equipment, but it is still an interesting place to explore.

Deep Shafts

Years ago copper and gold veins were developed southeast of the camp; some shafts reached a depth of over 200 feet. The main shafts, Copper King and the Golden Imp, were rumored to be rich, but how rich was never a matter of record. Here lived "Frenchie," another of the colorful individuals that traveled Mesquite Canyon. For years he carried a gun as insurance against the Gerbracht threat and carried a sizeable gold nugget to coax the unwary into investing in his gold mine.

Frenchie, in a battered pickup with his spotted dog Bowser, was a frequent and familiar sight as he headed in and out of Mesquite Canyon. He was the El Paso Mountains con-man supreme though not unique in the mining world. When he was broke, the gold nugget was sure to appear along with mining conversation. An eager investor would soon have verbal ownership, from one-tenth to one- half interest, in a gold mine. The extent of the investor's share depended upon his generosity. Probably no other gold mine in the Mojave Desert had as many half owners.

A Fall Feast

Though Frenchie's cabin is gone and the once neat yard now a mess of junk, brought in since the old miner departed this world, there is still one lone stand of Carizzo grass. Once abundant near desert springs it is now nearly extinct. Near the old pump house is a cluster of wild almond bushes that have survived. The scraggly, gray bush, a native of the area has small pink blooms in the spring that sends a perfumed message out to every wild bee within miles. In fall the nuts furnish a tasty feast for the ground squirrels, mice and pack rats.

Across the road from Colorado Camp is a bulldozed cut that reveals tan slate, rich red iron stain and gray to black chunks of coal. In 1898, 200 tons of low grade coal was mined here in three different shafts. It is reported to have been used locally to operate mining equipment and smelter operation. In the early 1900s the

Southern Pacific Railroad is said to have bought a sizeable amount and hauled it out to Mojave only to discover that it would hardly burn, much less produce enough heat to operate the steam locomotives.

The shafts caved in long ago and only coal that weathers out to the surface indicates where the operation existed. A search of the

Remains of the once-active Colorado Camp.

slate associated with the coal deposit will produce fossil casts of ancient tree limbs and leaves. Fern leaves are reputed to have been found at the 150 foot depth during the mining operation. A search of the surface coal could be worthwhile for a collector.

Passenger cars definitely should not go beyond Colorado Camp because the road develops sharp dips, high centers and ends above a deep cut in a short distance. Four-wheel drive vehicles can continue on for some distance by dropping down into a wash and squeezing past overhanging cliffs and narrow cuts. The view of Black Mountain from the camp site shows a jeep trail to the foot of the mountain and a foot path winding toward the top. For the hiker there are fossil wood and agate to collect; Indian trails, house rings and arrow chips are scattered along the way.

Burro Schmidt's Buried Treasure

Back track the short distance to within a few yards of the Gerbracht Camp sign, keeping to the right on EP 262 and EP 15 heading west. In about 0.7 miles a large silver-toned mine dump appears on the hill to the right across a wash. This area is known as the Copper Basin and the dump came from one of Burro Schmidt's mines. Opposite the dump and on the left side of the road is a small dug out area that once was the site of Schmidt's winter cabin. At his death the cabin was torn to shreds by friends who searched for his buried gold.

At this point there is a "Y" in the road. Take the road (EP 30) to the left at the sign "Tunnel" and make the gradual climb to the top of the mountain where Schmidt had his summer cabin and dug a tunnel that placed him in Ripley's Believe It or Not. The road is good and in 1.8 miles travelers are at another "Y." Take the road to the left following the signs to the "Tunnel" for 0.7 miles to the top of the mountain, and there the traveler will be greeted by Tonie Sieger, the present owner. There is a yard full of odds and ends, Schmidt's old cabin full of artifacts from his many mining years, and his mile long tunnel to explore.

Burro Schmidt came to California in 1894 for his health. The hot, dry desert air was the right answer. Though frail-appearing, he accomplished the monumental job of digging a tunnel through a mountain by hand. Sometimes he had burros or mules to pull ore cars of material to dump, but most of the time he not only did all the drilling, dynamiting and shoveling, but at the end of the day pushed the car of rubble to the entrance of his tunnel and a level area that is used for parking today. No one really knows why he spent half a lifetime digging a tunnel through a mountain, but there are many rumors. One rumor persists that there is a secret, sealed room off of the tunnel that is filled with gold from all his years of mining.

Coming back down the mountainside from the Burro Schmidt camp for 0.7 miles, take the left branch of EP 30 after leaving the gateway of poles in barrels. Within 1.4 miles from the camp the road dead ends into Last Chance Canyon road at a sign telling about the tunnel. This dead end faces Bonanza Gulch noted for the number of rich placer claims and a place where nuggets are still found. Upper Bonanza Gulch and Last Chance Canyon are another exploratory trip, so turn right onto EP 15 for 0.2 miles to Bickles Camp. Continue heading east for another 0.4 miles. A canyon to the left goes to Mesa Springs, once an Indian campsite around a water source; the road is rough and for four-wheel drive vehicles only.

Gold-Panning Possibilites

A tenth-of-a-mile farther is a passable road to the left that dead ends at a small primitive campsite. A tenth-of-a-mile farther along the main road is another trail to the left which goes into a larger camp area. This site has room for a number of campers without crowding. Unusual "mud-ball" formations add interest, old gold diggings are safe to explore and the wash offers gold panning or dry washing possibilities. It is a great place for children to run, climb and play miner in the shallow old diggings. What the early miner called these diggings has been lost through the years, but years ago we named it our Sandstone Cove, where it is pleasant even on the windiest, coldest winter day.

Go back to the main road (EP 30) the way you came in; the short cut to the left, EP 15 going to Mesa Springs and the camping area, is sandy beyond that point. Continue left or east on EP 30 and in less than two miles visitors are back at the Gerbracht Camp sign. Turn right onto EP 100 to Mesquite Canyon. In 3.5 miles the canyon road drops toward the valley bringing travelers out of the canyon through what geologists call "grabens." This is an ancient deposit of light colored, finely pulverized rock, now deeply eroded and topped by darker float. This is an unusual view of the result of vertical motion along the Garlock Fault. The fault itself runs about where the canyon road meets the hard surfaced Red Rock-Randsburg Road. From here Highway 395 is to the left and Highway 14 is to the right.

Before leaving the area take a few minutes and drive through the old town of Garlock. To get there, turn left at the junction of the Mesquite Canyon dirt road and the paved Red Rock-Randsburg Road for one mile and stay to the left at the "Y" as the road branches, with the right branch crossing the railroad tracks and going back to Randsburg. Staying to the left at the "Y" and one mile further are the ruins of the old town of Garlock.

Boom-Town Bonanza

Only a few structures and piles of rocks remain to mark the site of a once sizeable community that predates all other towns in the area. It started as an early day water and supply point for cattlemen and freighters who hauled borax out and supplies in. Gold miners and gold mills came in the 1890s to boom the small settlement into a town of importance with hotels, boarding houses, saloons, assayers, mine promoter offices, post office, Wells Fargo office and two to four stages a day.

The most pretentious building still standing is often mistaken for a bank, but was a saloon and bawdy house that probably handled more gold in a day than did the Wells Fargo office and the nearest bank. Main street crossed the present road and ran along the side of the saloon. A two-story hotel, the elite of the 1890s was the stage stop just opposite the saloon.

The walls of Jennie's Bar, that stood like a fortress for years, have succumbed to time and treasure hunters, and are now a heap of rock and adobe. An old Mexican-type arrastra, or drag mill, stands a short distance from the historical marker. Through this one was mechanized, instead of operated by a burro, it does show how boulders were dragged around and around to pulverize ore and release the gold. North of the arrastra is what was used as a blacksmith shop after the railroad began discarding broken ties. Still farther north are the remains of an old adobe home built in 1896.

The famous Garlock mill that processed the first gold from Randsburg's Yellow Aster Mine was close to the present railroad, but at the time of the mill operation all hauling was still dependent on teams. The site can be located by a rock foundation and a deep well which is fenced for the protection of visitors. Six mills were in operation until 1906 when the Yellow Aster built its own mill. Buildings and families moved up the hill to Randsburg where the new mill offered work for men.

Two and a half miles northeast on the paved road, a good dirt road to the left heads up Iron Canyon where abandoned mines, a few cabins belonging to weekend residents, and some new prospect holes add up to little of unusual interest to compensate for the drive. Hunters frequent the canyon in fall and gold prospectors avoiding the sand of Goler Wash come in this way and make a short hike down into the old Goler diggings.

Historic Goler Gulch, wash or canyon, by whatever term one chooses, is no longer an easy place to visit even for four-wheel drive vehicles. Loose sand has grown deeper by the year, waiting to be cleared out by a flash flood as happenes periodically. A couple of old cabins still stand along the bank but the famous gold diggings of the 1890s which ran for miles underground were filled and covered many years ago by a flood. Even the drainage system changed and the old landmarks are difficult to locate.

Finding Faults

A short distance beyond the cluster of tamarisk trees and the remains of a water pumping station, are the ruins of a mill high on the bank to the left of the road. The ditch between the road and the mill site is the Garlock Fault which has been running along the Garlock Road and crossing it at some points, but nowhere is it as easy to recognize as at this particular spot.

Three miles farther on there is a choice of going ahead one mile to Highway 395 or branching right on Goler Road to Randsburg and the highway. For bottle collectors the road to Randsburg offers the old Teagle loading platform near where the road crossed the railroad tracks. In the past it was a relatively untouched area to search that could produce sun-purpled liquor and medicine bottles as have been found at other freight stops along the tracks.

In the valley ahead are the leavings that were part of a gold dredge operation. The massive, rusting dredge had been sold for scrap, but where it operated is still much in evidence on the right side of the road. Here are the scars of a unique effort to form an artificial lake and float the dredge. Deep wells were put into operation to keep the lake filled, but more water evaporated into the air and leaked out through the sand in the bottom than stayed in the lake. Old time dry-wash miners had many good laughs at the expense of the metal monster that was so out of its element in the dry desert.

The road deadends at the top of the hill. To the left is Highway 395 or to the right the town of Randsburg, with it gold rich history and mining-camp legends.

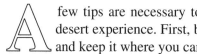

How to Enjoy Desert Exploring

To enjoy your desert ghost town travels to the fullest, make sure to keep these things in mind.

A few tips are necessary to ensure a pleasant, worry-free desert experience. First, bring your common sense along and keep it where you can put it to use at any time.

Just as one does for any trip, let family and friends know where you plan to explore and about when to expect you home.

Stay on traveled roads unless your vehicle is built for off-road travel and in case of a breakdown stay with your vehicle. Chances are good that another explorer will be along in a short time. Cross country hikes in a strange area, desert or not, is asking for trouble.

Be careful when climbing around mining areas. The ghost town desert is filled with open mine shafts, wells, tunnels and old buildings. Although they may be tempting to explore, they may also be unstable or crumbling. A bad spill or falling debris can spoil your trip.

Old mines and buildings are often home to other desert residents like snakes and scorpions. These creatures are usually as anxious to avoid you as you are them, so its just a matter of watching where you put your feet and hands. And be sure to look around before you sit down on a rock to eat a lunch or snack you packed.

Dress comfortably and take along extra warm items regardless of the time of year. Desert nights are cool and there can be a wide temperature variation in a short period of time. Walking boots have many advantages over shoes.

Carry a large container of water for you and your vehicle; desert dry air increases thirst. A first aid kit is a useful item for the back road explorer, too.

Take along more food than you can imagine eating, but don't be surprised if you consume it all. Fresh air and exploring builds an appetite.

Keep your gas tank filled and check your spare tire for air. Service stations are not on every corner and a spare tire that has lost air through months of disuse can spoil your day. Be sure you have a jack, too.

Desert roads are not freeways. Cut your speed, loaf along, see, feel and breath in the wonders of this world of many miles, varied faces and hidden values.

The desert is wonderful or dreadful, beautiful or bleak, exciting or dull, depending on you. Exercise caution and common sense, and above all respect Nature and your own physical limitations. These suggestions are the best insurance you have for a rewarding back-country experience.

An interesting array of mining equipment easily viewed from the road to Bickles Camp.

Bibliography

Bailey, Richard C. *Exploration in Kern*, Bakersfield, California: Kern County Historical Society, 1959.

Beebe, Lucius. *Mixed Train Daily*, New York: Dalton and Company, 1953.

Burmesiter, Eugene. *Early Days in Kern*. Bakersfield, California: Cordon House, 1963.

Caughey, John and Laree. *California Heritage*, Los Angeles, California: The Ward Ritchie Press, 1962.

Fenton, Carrol Lane and Mildred Adams. *The Fossil Book*, New York: Doubleday and Company, 1958.

Gudde, Erwin G. *California Place Names*, Berkeley, California: University of California Press, 1965.

Jaegar, Edmund C. *The California Desert*, Stanford, California: Stanford University Press, 1965.

Kern County Centennial Almanac, Bakersfield, California: Kern County Centennial Observance Committee, 1966.

Leadabrand, Russ. *A Guidebook to the Mojave Desert of California*, Los Angeles, California: The Ward Ritchie Press, 1966.

Leadabrand, Russ. *Exploring California Byways, Desert Country*, Los Angeles, California: The Ward Ritchie Press, 1969.

Munz, Philip A. *California Desert Wildflowers*, Berkeley, California: University of California Press, 1962.

Nadeau, Remi. *Ghost Towns and Mining Camps of California*, Los Angeles, California: The Ward Ritchie Press, 1967.

Peirson, Emma. *Kern's Desert*, Bakersfield, California: Kern County Historical Society, 1956.

Shelton, John S. *Geology Illustrated*, San Francisco, California: W. H. Freeman Company, 1966.

Starry, Roberta M. *Gold Gamble*, China Lake, California: Maturango Museum, 1974.

Troxel, B.W. and Morton, P.K. *Mines and Mineral Resources of Kern County, California*, San Francisco, California: California Division of Mines and Geology, 1962.

Twisselmann, Earnest C. *A Flora of Kern County, California*, San Francisco, California: University of San Francisco, 1967.

Vanders, Iris and Kerr, Paul F. *Mineral Recognition*, New York: John Wiley and Sons Inc., 1967.

Wright, Laura and Troxel, B. W. *Geology of Southern California, Western Mojave Desert and Death Valley Region*, San Francisco, California: California Division of Mines, 1954.

Wynn, Marcia Rittenhouse. *Desert Bonanza*, Los Angeles, California: Arthur H. Clark Company, 1963.

Index

Atolia,*1,6,7,37,38,60,61, 66,67,78,79,80,91*

Baltic Mill,*17*
Barker Mill,*38,79*
Ben Hur Mine,*88*
Bickle's Camp,*99*
Big Butte Mine,*16,83,86*
Big Dyke Mine,*16*
Black Mountain,*23,96,98*
Blackwater Ranch,*61*
Bonanza Gulch,*99*
Buckboard Mine,*39,90,91*
Burcham, Charles,*3*
Burma Road,*15*
Butte Avenue,*14,15,16,80,86*

California City,*8,47,80*
California City Blvd.,*47*
Cantil,*7*
Carson and Colorado Railroad,*8*
Cerro Gordo Mine,*5,45*
Colorado Camp,*96,97,98*
Consolidated Mine,*86*
Copper Basin,*99*
Copper King Mine,*97*
Cow Wells,*4*
Cuddeback Dry Lake,*62, 63,90*

Death Valley,*2,4,5,8,17,48, 70,74,75,83*
Decker Mine,*95*
Desert Tortoise Discovery Center,*31,47,48*
Dos Pecannini Mine,*16*
Dutch Cleanser Mine, *21,25,26,30,32*

El Paso Mountains, *2,35,42,83,90,93,96,97*

Fiddler's Gulch,*16,86*
Fremont,*60,67,78*
Fremont, John C.,*60*
Fremont Peak,*59,60,61, 62,63,64,65,66,67,77,78*
Fremont Valley,*2,4,89,90,94*
Frenchie, French C.C.,*97*

Galileo Peak,*47,48*
Garlock,*4,7,29,37,41,81, 100,101,102*
Garlock, Eugene,*4*
Garlock Fault,*100,102*
Garlock Road,*102*
Gerbracht Camp,*96,98,100*
G.B. Mine, Gold Bug,*88*
Glamis Gold Inc.,*7,17*
Gold Coin Mine,*88*
Gold Crown Mine,*88*
Gold King Mine,*88*
Golden Badger Mine,*95*
Golden Eagle Mine,*88,96*
Golden Imp Mine,*97*
Golden Valley,*59,90*
Goler,*2,3,4,5,7,9,37,41,54,101*

Goler Road,*102*
Government Peak,*86,87, 89,90*
Grubstake Hill,*26*

Hamburger Mill,*64*
Hard Cash Mine,*16*
Harrison's Saloon,*83*
Hatfield,*23*
Hinkley,*65*
Hoffman Road,*62,63,65,66*
Holly Cleanser Mine,*21,23,*

Inn City,*6,81*
Iron Canyon,*101*

Johannesburg,*1,4,5,6,7,17,49, 67,81,82*

Kelly Silver Mine,*36,79,80, 81,86*
King Solomon Mine,*83*
Koehn, Charles,*5*
Koehn Dry Lake,*42,90*
Kramer Junction,*7,8,60, 67,77,78*

Last Chance Canyon,*19,21, 23,30,32,96,99*
Lexington Avenue,*15,16*
Little Butte Mine,*15*
Lockhart,*65,66*

McGowan's Gold Mine,*96*
Mt. Wells Road,*83*
Mesa Springs,*99,100*
Mesquite Canyon,*93,94, 97,100*
Mesquite Springs,*93*
Miner's Dream Mine,*16*
Mojave,*7,8,43,57*
Monarch Rand Mine,*67*
Mooers, F.M.,*3*
Myrick, Shady,*83*

Neuralia Road,*46*

Old Look Out Mine,*95*
Old Spanish Mine,*79*
Opera House,*14*
Orphan Girl Mine,*88*
Osdick,*6,81*
Osdick, Pete,*81*
Osdick Road,*49,79,80,82,86*
Owl Saloon,*82*

Panamint,*4,5,57*
Panamint Street,*83*
Pearl Wedge Mine,*88*
Pinnacles,*34,69,73,74,75*

Rand Camp,*4,11,16*
Rand Mining Company,*7,16, 17,86,87,88,89,90*
Rand Mountains,*4,5, 85, 87,89*
Rand Road,*83*
Rand Street,*17*

Randsburg,*1,3,4,5,6,7,12,17,27, 40,49,57,60,81,83,86,94, 100,101,102*
Randsburg Bank,*14*
Randsburg Loop Road,*17,86*
Randsburg-Mojave Road, *31,35,38,47,48,80,86, 87, 89,91*
Randsburg Railroad,*5,8,60*
Red Bird Mine,*88*
Red Mountain*1,6,7,36,38,40, 53,55,60,69,70,75,77,79, 82,86*
Red Mountain Road, *17,80,82,86*
Red Rock Canyon,*5,19, 31,43,45,46*
Red Rock Canyon State Park, *19,21,23,24,25,43,46*
Red Rock Railroad,*46*
Red Rock-Randsburg Road, *19,20,26,43,60,94,100*
Ridgecrest,*7,8,75*

Santa Fe Railroad,*67,77,79*
Schmidt, Burro,*83,99*
Schmidt Tunnel,*20,99*
Searles Dry Lake,*57,69,74*
Searles Station,*8*
Side Hill Wedge Mine,*95*
Sieger, Tonie,*99*
Silver Dollar Saloon,*82*
Silver Saddle Ranch Resort, *47,48*
Sin City,*6,81*
Singleton, John,*3*
Sophie Moren Mine,*88*
Southern Pacific Railroad, *8,26,33,51,56,57,71,98*
Spangler,*72,73*
St. Charles Hotel, *83*
St. Elmo,*78*
Still Lower Half Mine,*96*
Stringer District,*39,86,91*
Summit Diggings,*3,5,9,33, 51,54,57*
Sunshine Mine,*86,87,88,89*

Tam-O-Shanter Mine,*88*
Teagle's Store,*83*
Trona,*7,8,69,70,72,75*
Trona Railroad,*71,75*
Trona Road,*70,71,72,73,75*
Twin Brothers Mine,*96*

Union Mine,*38*
Upper Bonanza Gulch,*22,23,32*

Victory Wedge Mine,*88*

White House Saloon,*13*
Windy Mine,*17,40*
Winnie Mine,*88*

Yarbrough Gold and Silver Company,*93*
Yellow Aster Mine,*4,6,7,13, 15,16,27,28,29,85,101*

106